Implementing
FRBR
in Libraries

Key Issues and Future Directions

Yin Zhang and Athena Salaba

Neal-Schuman Publishers, Inc.
New York   London

Published by Neal-Schuman Publishers, Inc.
100 William St., Suite 2004
New York, NY 10038

Printed and bound in the United States of America.

The paper used in this publication meets the minimum requirements of American National Standard for Information Sciences–Permanence of Paper for Printed Library Materials, ANSI Z39.48-1992.

Library of Congress Cataloging-in-Publication Data

Zhang, Yin, 1965-
    Implementing FRBR in libraries : key issues and future directions / Yin Zhang and Athena Salaba.
        p. cm.
    Includes bibliographical references and index.
    ISBN 978-1-55570-661-6 (alk. paper)
    1. FRBR (Conceptual model) I. Salaba, Athena. II. Title.

Z666.6.Z48 2009
025.3—dc22
                                                    2009031729

CONTENTS

List of Illustrations   vii

Preface   ix

Acknowledgments   xiii

Chapter 1. Introduction to FRBR   1

What Is FRBR?   1

Why Was FRBR Introduced?   3

What Are the Potential Benefits of Implementing
    FRBR?   4

What Is the Current Status of FRBR Development?   8

What Are the Most Critical and Challenging Issues
    Facing FRBR Development?   9

Summary   10

References   10

Chapter 2. The FRBR Model   13

The FRBR Model: Entity Groups   14

Further Development of the FRBR Model   23

The FRBR Model Family: FRAD and FRSAD   25

Interoperability with Other Models   28

Critical Issues and Challenges in the FRBR Model   28

References   30

**Chapter 3. Impact of FRBR on Current Cataloging
Standards and Practice**   33

What Changes Will FRBR Bring?   34

International Cataloguing Principles   34

Description Standards   35
Changes in Encoding Standards   41
Are Changes in Cataloging Practice Coming Soon?   45
Critical Issues and Challenges in Cataloging Standards
   and Practice   50
Summary   51
References   52

Chapter 4. FRBR Application   **57**
Collections: Genre/Format and Disciplinary
   Communities   58
Settings   67
Critical Issues and Challenges in FRBR Application   70
Summary   71
References   71

Chapter 5. FRBR Implementations in Library Catalogs   **75**
Current FRBR Implementation Projects   76
Overview of FRBR Implementation Projects   91
Critical Issues and Challenges in FRBR Implementations   97
Summary   104
References   105

Chapter 6. FRBR Research   **109**
FRBR Research Overview   109
Gaps in FRBR User Research   112
Critical Issues and Challenges in FRBR Research   117
Summary   119
References   120

Chapter 7. Conclusions and Future Directions for FRBR   **123**
FRBR Development   123
Key FRBR Issues   126
Future Directions for FRBR   128

Concluding Remarks   131
References   132

Appendix A. Acronyms   135
Appendix B. FRBR Implementation Examples   139

Index   147
About the Authors   153

LIST OF ILLUSTRATIONS

Figure 2-1   Group 1 Entities and Their Primary
             Relationships   15

Figure 2-2   *Harry Potter* in FRBR Group 1 View   16

Figure 2-3   Group 1 and Group 2 Relationships   18

Figure 2-4   FRBR Subject Relationship   20

Figure 3-1   Model A: Using Authority Records for
             Work/Expression   47

Figure 3-2   Model B: Using Bibliographic Records for
             Work/Expression   48

Figure 5-1   An Example of a WorldCat.org Search Result
             Display   78

Figure 5-2   An Example of the UCLA Cinema Search
             Result Display for a Work   79

Figure 5-3   An Example of UCLA Cinema Expression
             and Manifestation Records   80

Figure 5-4   The OCLC FictionFinder Search Result
             Display by Work   81

Figure 5-5   The OCLC FictionFinder FRBR View of a Work
             and Its Expressions and Manifestations   82

Figure 5-6   A Record of Shakespeare's *Hamlet* with FRBR
             Display Hyperlink   83

Figure 5-7   The FRBR-like Display of the Record Clusters
             for Shakespeare's *Hamlet*   83

Figure 5-8   Shakespeare's *Hamlet* in English Books
             in FRBR Display   84

Table 7-1   Most Critical FRBR Issues Overall   127

PREFACE

There is no doubt that the information environment which libraries operate in today and will operate in for the foreseeable future is quite different from the one that existed a half century ago. Current cataloging standards, practices, and library catalogs based on the information environment from decades ago are facing great challenges in meeting users' information needs and facilitating information seeking in an increasingly electronic environment. These challenges, facing both libraries and their users, are urgent and real. Many people believe that if library-based finding systems don't evolve quickly, they will be replaced by Internet-based search engines.

The library community has actively debated the future of library catalogs as well as changes in cataloging standards and practices for decades. In an effort to address both changes in the information environment and related challenges, in 1998 the International Federation of Library Associations and Institutions (IFLA) published *Functional Requirements for Bibliographic Records* (FRBR), which presented a new conceptual model of the bibliographic universe with a strong user focus. The library community embraced FRBR and has actively explored its potential benefits for library professionals and library end users alike.

A decade after FRBR's official publication, and despite much lively discussion, creative exploration, practical development, and active research about FRBR, it is still unclear to many how this model may be effectively applied to the process of cataloging, how cataloging-related standards and practices will be changed, and how information systems may be improved to better meet user needs and support information seeking in today's ever changing information environment.

Implementing FRBR in Libraries: Key Issues and Future Directions is designed to bring answers in three ways:

▶ to provide an overview of the current status of FRBR development,

▶ to identify the key FRBR issues that need to be addressed, and

▶ to point to future directions of FRBR development.

The book's overall organization parallels these goals. The introductory Chapter 1 provides a brief background and overview of FRBR by addressing several important questions: What is FRBR? Why was it introduced? What are the potential benefits of implementing FRBR? What is the current status of FRBR development? What are the most critical and challenging issues facing FRBR development? This chapter serves as a basis for further discussion regarding the various FRBR developmental fronts covered in the subsequent chapters.

Chapter 2 provides a detailed description of the FRBR model and its components, illustrating the entities and their relationships and giving an account of its evolving nature, including developments proposed after FRBR's publication. This chapter also offers a discussion on other IFLA models linked to FRBR, efforts to harmonize the FRBR model with other conceptual models, and model-related issues. Chapter 3 discusses how the FRBR model may influence and transform description standards as well as cataloging and metadata practices, current standard development, and necessary changes for the near future.

The next two chapters showcase examples of how FRBR has been applied and implemented, and they present and discuss related issues. Specifically, Chapter 4 provides an overview of current FRBR applications in various settings (in traditional libraries, digital libraries, consortia), and with regard to resources in various media and disciplines. Chapter 5 reviews various efforts that explore methods for implementing the FRBR model to create more effective library catalogs. The chapter covers examples and discussions of various implementation approaches and FRBR implementation projects that have involved development of FRBR–based systems, algorithms, and software for FRBR implementation.

Chapter 6 provides a brief overview of research efforts related to all FRBR developmental fronts with an additional focus on gaps in FRBR user research and other critical areas that require immediate attention. Chapter 7 presents a unified overview of FRBR, issues, and future directions of FRBR development.

Two appendixes are included to provide supporting information. Since there are a large number of acronyms related to FRBR, Appendix A offers a comprehensive list of acronyms to aid readers new to the field; Appendix B provides a collective list of FRBR implementation examples referenced in various chapters.

This book was designed to meet the needs of the following audiences:

1. Library professionals, such as catalogers, indexers, and metadata librarians who need to know the latest state of the model's application, current issues that need to be addressed, and changes in descriptive standards and practices

2. Library and other information agency administrators who need to be aware of the changes in practice and system development to better plan and manage resources

3. Reference librarians who need to know how a FRBR–based catalog will improve their ability to more effectively help end users

4. System developers and vendors who need to be aware of the implementations and tools that have been developed and tested thus far for future development

5. Researchers and practitioners who need to know the latest developments in the FRBR model, its theoretical framework, and the most important issues that need to be explored and systematically examined

6. Library and information science faculty and students who need a comprehensive account of all aspects of the FRBR model

FRBR offers libraries a new perspective and a broader view of the bibliographic universe capable of meeting the challenges facing both libraries and library users. FRBR shows great potential to help develop better systems for users, improve cataloging efforts, and better manage resources in a digital environment. Because of this potential, it is important that library professionals continue to work to better understand FRBR, keep current with its developments, and be aware of the related issues and future directions in implementing it in libraries. *Implementing FRBR in Libraries: Key Issues and Future Directions* is intended to fulfill this need.

ACKNOWLEDGMENTS

This book would not have been possible without the dedication of and contributions by all the individuals who have been involved in Functional Requirements for Bibliographic Records (FRBR) development and who have laid the foundational work for FRBR. In particular, we would like to thank the individuals who participated in the Delphi Study and contributed their expertise and insight toward raising and evaluating the critical FRBR issues in current and future developments.

We thank the Institute of Museum and Library Services (IMLS) for funding the three-year project on which this book is based and Kent State University for the matching and supplemental funding for the project. We are grateful to the project's advisory team for their advice and support: Barbara Tillett from the Library of Congress and Online Computer Library Center (OCLC) researchers Edward T. O'Neill, Diane Vizine-Goetz, and Thomas B. Hickey. We also thank Martha M. Yee for her insight on the UCLA Film and Television Archive OPAC.

Special thanks go to Charles Harmon for his inspiration, which started us on the journey of writing this book, to Sandy Wood for her support and patience along the way, and to other Neal-Schuman staff for their creative work. Thanks must also go to the anonymous reviewer of the manuscript for the valuable and constructive comments and suggestions for revisions and improvements.

We appreciate the technical support given by Lei Xie, North Lilly, and Edward Farnbauch in our FRBR implementation efforts and the research support for the project and writing of this book from our current and former graduate assistants: Jake Schaub, Vicki Ceci, Theda Schwing, Lee Zickel, Beth Fleming, Matt Shreffler, Jamie Davis, and Amanda Duca.

Finally, we would like to thank our colleagues at the School of Library and Information Science for their support and our families for their love, understanding, and sacrifice.

INTRODUCTION TO FRBR

This introductory chapter provides a brief background and overview of the Functional Requirements for Bibliographic Records (FRBR) by addressing several important questions: What is FRBR? Why was it introduced? What are the potential benefits of implementing FRBR? What is the current status of FRBR development? What are the most critical and challenging issues facing FRBR development? Answers to these questions will provide a broad picture of the FRBR landscape and will serve as a basis for further discussion regarding the various areas of FRBR development, which will be covered in the individual chapters of this book.

WHAT IS FRBR?

In 1998, the International Federation of Library Associations and Institutions (IFLA) published *Functional Requirements for Bibliographic Records: Final Report*, which introduced FRBR as a new conceptual model to represent the bibliographic universe (International Federation of Library Associations and Institutions Study Group, 1998). The FRBR model was developed based on an entity-relationship analysis that is commonly used for the conceptual design of relational databases. The purpose of this entity-relationship analysis was to discover the logical nature of the bibliographic data in terms of the following elements:

▶ *Entities:* key objects, such as works, persons, and concepts that users are interested in when using bibliographic information. These objects contain bibliographic data (e.g., title of the work, name of person, and term for the concept) that help users to find, identify, select, and obtain what they are looking for.

▶ *Attributes* or *characteristics:* bibliographic data with which entities are associated. In FRBR, attributes are entity-specific, and the model offers a list of attributes associated with each entity. For example, the work entity's attributes include title, form, date, other distinguishing characteristics, intended termination, intended audience, context, medium of performance (musical work), numeric designation (musical work), key (musical work), coordinates (cartographic work), and equinox (cartographic work). In general, attributes offer ways for users to search bibliographic systems such as catalogs and to seek information about a particular entity.

▶ *Relationships:* associations or connections between two or more entities. For example, *work* and *person* entities can be associated through a "created by" authorship relationship.

Collectively, FRBR entities, attributes, and relationships can be used to represent the complex bibliographic universe. At its core, FRBR was developed with a strong user focus by clearly defining four generic user tasks for using bibliographic information: *find, identify, select,* and *obtain.* Such user focus is reflected in the definitions of key concepts in the FRBR model:

▶ *Entities* are "key objects that are of interest to users of information in a particular domain" (International Federation of Library Associations and Institutions Study Group, 1998: 3).

▶ Entity *attributes* and *relationships* are "most important to users in formulating bibliographic searches, interpreting responses to those searches, and 'navigating' the universe of entities described in bibliographic records" (International Federation of Library Associations and Institutions Study Group, 1998: 3).

▶ "Each attribute and relationship can be mapped directly to the user tasks they support" (International Federation of Library Associations and Institutions Study Group, 1998: 79).

It is important to note that *users,* as defined in the FRBR model, include various user groups: library patrons and staff, publishers, distributors, retailers, and providers and users of information services outside the traditional library setting.

Essentially, FRBR is a conceptual model, a framework, and a new user-focused perspective through which one can view the bibliographic universe at an abstract level, which might explain why understanding FRBR in practical terms poses a challenge. There has been literature devoted to explaining the model (e.g., Maxwell, 2008; Carlyle, 2006; Tillett, 2005b). A more detailed review and discussion of the FRBR model, provided in Chapter 2, will help develop an understanding of the model and its development.

WHY WAS FRBR INTRODUCED?

The current cataloging principles and standards, such as the Paris Principles, the International Standard Bibliographic Descriptions (ISBDs), and national and international cataloging codes, represent the subsequent outcome of the IFLA-led international effort to reexamine cataloging theories and practices initiated in the late 1950s. Since this foundational work was conducted, the operational aspect of the cataloging environment has undergone drastic changes driven by the following key factors (International Federation of Library Associations and Institutions Study Group, 1998):

▶ Technological advances that support computer creation and processing of bibliographic data as well as shared contribution and use of bibliographic data at national and international levels

▶ Economic pressures faced by libraries to reduce cataloging costs while an increasing amount and new types of materials arrive for processing

▶ Libraries' "user awareness" and the necessity of meeting increasing user expectations and needs

As part of the endeavor to address the challenges facing libraries and to respond to the changing environment, IFLA commissioned members who served in IFLA's Section on Cataloging and Section on Classification and Indexing for a three-year FRBR study, with the following two primary objectives:

The first is to provide a clearly defined, structured framework for relating the data that are recorded in bibliographic records to the needs of the users of those records. The second objective is to recommend a basic level of functionality for records created by national bibliographic agencies. (International Federation of Library Associations and Institutions Study Group, 1998: 7)

The FRBR model is the result of this study, which included a worldwide, open peer review. A detailed account of the origins of the model is available in the official FRBR report (International Federation of Library Associations and Institutions Study Group, 1998) and in an article by the study group's chair, Olivia Madison (Madison, 2005), which covers details about the historical context of the FRBR study, the study process, the team members involved, the project charge assigned to the team, and some key issues that arose throughout the study.

WHAT ARE THE POTENTIAL BENEFITS OF IMPLEMENTING FRBR?

FRBR offers a new perspective and a broader view of the bibliographic universe, providing abundant opportunities for libraries to develop catalogs that function more effectively and provide better user services during the process of accessing bibliographic data in an information environment that is becoming increasingly electronic. Although FRBR is a conceptual model and its practical applications and implementations are currently still in an early, exploratory stage, some major benefits of introducing FRBR into libraries have been identified and suggested, including those explained in the following sections.

FRBR Helps Develop Better Systems for Users

The strong user focus of FRBR has been cited as a benefit for designing better information systems because the knowledge of the users and uses of the information system helps in making informed decisions on system design options (Riva, 2007). FRBR can serve as a framework that promises a profound influence on the development of bibliographic systems with expanded contents and access (Madison, 2006; Tillett, 2005b). Specifically, FRBR offers possible solutions toward developing effective online catalogs and retrieval tools that truly support user information tasks. Examples of possible improvements may include the following:

- ▶ Addressing common problems users have when searching in current catalogs for materials with a known author and title (Yee, 2005). For example, current catalogs do not effectively support a search for a particular work using a combination of an author's name and a title, nor do current catalogs effectively support searches that involve names or titles that have changed.

- ▶ Providing better indexing for searches and display of search results for entities such as works, expressions, and manifestations (Yee, 2005). Current online catalogs do not support users in their attempt to find a list of all expressions and manifestations of a work and related works. Users need to search and make their own collocation decisions.

- ▶ Supporting a more meaningful search process with hierarchical displays and navigations for searching and browsing. The hierarchical display and navigation could result in possible simplification of information seeking through "information hiding" of irrelevant entities and attributes (Mimno, Crane, and Jones, 2005; Noerr et al., 1998).

- ▶ Enhancing current library catalogs for better searching, retrieval, and display by collocating records based on various bibliographic relationships (Dickey, 2008). The relationships among various entities defined in the FRBR model can serve as a basis for collocation at the entity level, while current catalogs support collocation largely based on attributes. The FRBR relationships can also be used for designing visual tools to facilitate information seeking in the bibliographic universe.

- ▶ Taking full advantage of digital technologies to associate bibliographic records for better navigation and collocation, which is particularly important in resource sharing environments where collections tend to be larger (Gonzalez, 2005).

FRBR Helps Improve Cataloging Efforts

One of the key factors that drove the creation of FRBR was the desire of libraries to address the challenges of cataloging in an operational environment that had changed as a result of the factors mentioned in the previous section of this chapter. FRBR has indeed been recognized as being "likely to induce profound changes in cataloguers' landscape" (Le Boeuf, 2001: 15) and "if fully implemented, FRBR would produce the biggest change cataloging has seen in the last century" (Online Computer Library Center, 2003). Some of the specific identified benefits of implementing FRBR for cataloging include the following:

- ▶ Achieving higher quality and more effectively shared cataloging efforts with easier maintenance (Noerr et al., 1998). The hierarchical structure of Group 1 entities (work, expression, manifestation, and item) allows assignment of bibliographic data elements to entities at various levels in the hierarchy. As a result, creating a record at a lower level in the hierarchy does not need to repeat the data that has been available in records above the record's level in the hierarchy. Therefore, duplicate cataloging efforts could be reduced, inconsistency from duplication could be decreased, and more shared cataloging could be possible.

- ▶ Reducing cataloging effort by doing "minimal level" cataloging with a clear evaluation and reexamination of the relationship between individual data elements in the record and the needs of the user (International Federation of Library Associations and Institutions Study Group, 1998). Besides the hierarchical structure of Group 1 entities mentioned previously, which allows minimal level cataloging data in each record, FRBR also allows a minimum set of distinct entities needed for the bibliographic universe in the model, which can help reduce cataloging effort.

- ▶ Sharing data in existing authority records and bibliographic records based on bibliographic relationships that may lead to new models of bibliographic structures (Tillett, 2005b). FRBR offers an opportunity to reevaluate the data assignment between authority records and bibliographic records. For example, subject headings and classification could be included in the authority record for the work instead of redundantly in the bibliographic record for each manifestation.

▶ Facilitating international standardization and reducing costs for cataloging on a global scale by minimizing duplicate cataloging effort (Tillett, 2005b; International Federation of Library Associations and Institutions Study Group, 1998). FRBR has been embraced by library and related communities worldwide, which will facilitate collaboration and development of international standards for more effective cataloging.

FRBR Helps Better Manage Resources in a Digital Environment

FRBR will help foster easier integration of resources and systems among libraries and beyond in the digital information environment because it was created considering a wide range of materials, media, and formats such as textual, cartographic, audiovisual, graphic, three-dimensional, and film (International Federation of Library Associations and Institutions Study Group, 1998). For example, although the process is still challenging, FRBR can help integrate library catalogs with tools for archives and museums since it can be extended to other disciplines and applied to library-related institutions (Noerr et al., 1998). It is believed that FRBR can contribute toward the future integration of "all resources in all of the world's repositories, including libraries, bookstores, music and film archives, publishing houses, etc." (Tillett, 2005a: 202). At the same time, FRBR offers a framework that helps develop systems that may support the searching of "all potential sources of information" because FRBR, in combination with its expansion FRAD (Functional Requirements for Authority Data), could enable increased interoperability and accessibility to bibliographic data and items (Tillett, 2005a: 202).

Because of the extent of the potential benefits and opportunities created by introducing FRBR into libraries and other institutions and settings, it is a topic that is too significant to ignore. Since its inception, FRBR has been embraced by the library community and continues to shape the direction of future cataloging rules and related standards and, consequently, library practices and system development. A detailed discussion of the impact of FRBR on current cataloging standards and practices and specific examples of FRBR-related applications, implementations, and research activities will be provided in the subsequent chapters of this book. Such examples and discussion will illustrate what has been done in exploring the opportunities FRBR may offer and will suggest ideas as to what libraries and institutions may possibly do to incorporate FRBR.

WHAT IS THE CURRENT STATUS OF FRBR DEVELOPMENT?

FRBR development can be characterized as dynamic, rapidly evolving, and interdisciplinary. Major developmental fronts are underway in the following areas:

- ▶ Review, evaluation, revision, and expansion of the FRBR model itself
- ▶ Creation and revision of standards related to FRBR
- ▶ Application of FRBR in various collections, settings, and disciplines
- ▶ Development of FRBR-based systems, algorithms, and software
- ▶ Conducting research in the above areas and FRBR user studies

A detailed account of each developmental front will be covered in subsequent chapters in this book. It should be noted that in the current literature, FRBR application and implementation both refer to the efforts that involve exploring and applying the FRBR model to organize, manage, and provide access to collections of resources. These efforts include both theoretical and practical discussions as well as the actual creation of working products. In this book, however, a distinction is made between FRBR application and FRBR implementation due to the large amount of literature on these two topics. Specifically, FRBR application will refer to efforts that focus more on the theoretical and practical discussions of how to apply the model in various settings, collections, and disciplines, while FRBR implementation will refer to efforts dealing with the actual creation and development of working FRBR-based systems, algorithms, and software tools and utilities.

WHAT ARE THE MOST CRITICAL AND CHALLENGING ISSUES FACING FRBR DEVELOPMENT?

After a decade of discussion, exploration, and development, a better understanding of FRBR is still needed. The full potential of FRBR and its impact on library communities and beyond remain to be seen. Additionally, a clear direction for future FRBR research, application, and implementation still needs to be established. In spring of 2007, to better identify critical issues and challenges within FRBR research and practice, the authors of this book conducted a three-round survey with a group of 33 FRBR experts as part of a three-year Institute of Museum and Library Services (IMLS)–funded project concerning the research and development of FRBR-based retrieval systems (Zhang and Salaba, 2007).

The selected experts met at least one of the following criteria: (1) had published materials on FRBR, (2) had served in FRBR review groups, or (3) had been directly involved in FRBR system development projects. During the three rounds of surveys, the study used the Delphi method to engage the FRBR experts first in identifying critical issues, then, during follow-up rounds, in rating the importance of those issues by reviewing the summarized results from immediately previous rounds. All expert input was individual, anonymous, and shared among the group after each round in order to generate new ideas in the following round and to reach group consensus. This issue-raising and consensus-building process helped identify the most critical issues for future FRBR research and practice in each of the five FRBR developmental fronts. These issues will be presented and discussed in their respective chapters in this book in the section titled "Critical Issues and Challenges." Other details of the Delphi study are reported in "What Is Next for FRBR? A Delphi Study" (Zhang and Salaba, 2009).

SUMMARY

FRBR is a new conceptual model of the bibliographic universe that offers great potential benefits to various user groups, including both end users and library and information professionals, in the increasingly digital information environment. This chapter has outlined the major FRBR developmental fronts and related critical issues to be covered in individual chapters in this book. The rest of the book will present a current, integrated, and systematic view of FRBR that is supported by current literature, practice examples, research, and results generated from the Delphi study.

REFERENCES

Carlyle, Allyson. 2006. "Understanding FRBR As a Conceptual Model: FRBR and the Bibliographic Universe." *Library Resources & Technical Services* 50, no. 4: 264–273.

Dickey, Timothy J. 2008. "FRBRization of a Library Catalog: Better Collocation of Records, Leading to Enhanced Search, Retrieval, and Display." *Information Technology & Libraries* 27, no. 1: 23–32.

Gonzalez, Linda. 2005. "What Is FRBR?" *Library Journal netConnect* (Spring): 12, 14.

International Federation of Library Associations and Institutions, Study Group on the Functional Requirements for Bibliographic Records. 1998. *Functional Requirements for Bibliographic Records: Final Report.* Munich, Germany: K. G. Saur. Available: www.ifla.org/en/publications/functional-requirements-for-bibliographic-records (accessed July 30, 2009).

Le Boeuf, Patrick. 2001. "FRBR and Further." *Cataloging & Classification Quarterly* 32, no. 4: 15–52.

Madison, Olivia M. A. 2005. "The Origins of the IFLA Study on Functional Requirements for Bibliographic Records." *Cataloging & Classification Quarterly* 39, no. 3/4: 15–37.

Madison, Olivia M. A. 2006. "Utilizing the FRBR Framework in Designing User-Focused Digital Content and Access Systems." *Library Resources & Technical Services* 50, no. 1: 10–15.

Maxwell, Robert L. 2008. *FRBR: A Guide for the Perplexed.* Chicago: American Library Association.

Mimno, David, Gregory Crane, and Alison Jones. 2005. "Hierarchical Catalog Records: Implementing a FRBR Catalog." *D-Lib Magazine* 11, no. 10. Available: www.dlib.org/dlib/october05/crane/10crane.html (accessed July 30, 2009).

Noerr, Peter, Paula Goossens, Dan Matei, Petra Otten, Susanna Peruginelli, and Maria Witt. 1998. "User Benefits from a New Bibliographic Model: Follow-Up of the IFLA Functional Requirements Study." *International Cataloguing and Bibliographic Control: Quarterly Bulletin of the IFLA UBCIM Programme* 28, no. 3: 80–81. Available: http://archive.ifla.org/IV/ifla64/084-126e.htm (accessed July 30, 2009).

Online Computer Library Center. 2003. "OCLC Research Activities and IFLA's Functional Requirements for Bibliographic Records." Available: www.oclc.org/us/en/par/default.htm (accessed July 30, 2009).

Riva, Pat. 2007. "Introducing the Functional Requirements for Bibliographic Records and Related IFLA Developments." *Bulletin of the American Society for Information Science and Technology* 33, no. 6: 7–11.

Tillett, Barbara B. 2005a. "FRBR and Cataloging for the Future." *Cataloging & Classification Quarterly* 39, no. 3/4: 197–205.

Tillett, Barbara B. 2005b. "What Is FRBR? A Conceptual Model for the Bibliographic Universe." *The Australian Library Journal* 54, no. 1: 24–30.

Yee, Martha M. 2005. "FRBRization: A Method for Turning Online Public Finding Lists into Online Public Catalogs." *Information Technology and Libraries* 24, no. 2: 77–95.

Zhang, Yin, and Athena Salaba. 2007. "FRBR-Based Systems to Effectively Support User Tasks and Facilitate Information Seeking." Available: http://frbr.slis.kent.edu (accessed July 30, 2009).

Zhang, Yin, and Athena Salaba. 2009. "What Is Next for FRBR? A Delphi Study." *The Library Quarterly* 79, no. 2: 233–255.

THE FRBR MODEL

This chapter is designed to investigate the FRBR (Functional Requirements for Bibliographic Records) model itself, its components, developments proposed after its publication, benefits and issues related to the model, a discussion of other IFLA (International Federation of Library Associations and Institutions) models linked to FRBR, and efforts to harmonize it with other conceptual models.

In 1992 IFLA approved the terms of reference for the newly created study group chaired by Olivia Madison tasked with studying the functional requirements for bibliographic records. The final report, titled the *Functional Requirements for Bibliographic Records,* was produced, reviewed, and then approved in 1997 (Madison, 2005). FRBR is a conceptual model of the bibliographic universe as represented in library catalogs through descriptions (bibliographic records). FRBR presents a theoretical representation that aims to provide a simplified description of a very complex environment. This environment includes bibliographic records that store data, the cataloging process for creating these records, and the catalog itself, which provides access to the resources described in the records when end users interact with this tool. As a conceptual model, FRBR does not provide guidance or a set of rules for creating these descriptions but can serve as a basis for the creation of rules for description. As is stated in the FRBR report, the goal of the FRBR study was to develop "a framework that would provide a clear, precisely stated, and commonly shared understanding of what it is that the bibliographic record aims to provide information about" (International Federation of Library Associations and Institutions Study Group, 1998: 2).

Specifically, FRBR is an entity-relationship (ER) conceptual model. This particular type of conceptual modeling allows for the identification of major objects or entities and a set of attributes characterizing each entity. In addition, it identifies and defines the relationships that exist among the entities. However, FRBR goes beyond the ER model in that it also identifies user tasks. It examines the type of tasks with which a user approaches the catalog, or ways a user might use the catalog and its information (attributes and relationships) to find a certain entity or a set of entities. To help link the user tasks to the entity-relationship model, FRBR provides mappings between tasks and entity attributes and relationships as defined in the model.

THE FRBR MODEL: ENTITY GROUPS

FRBR identifies a total of ten entities categorized into three entity groups. The first group is labeled **Group 1** and represents the products of intellectual or artistic endeavors. In other words, it is all of the resources to which we provide access through our catalogs. The following four entities are included in Group 1:

▶ *Work:* a distinct intellectual or artistic creation

▶ *Expression:* the intellectual or artistic realization of a *work*

▶ *Manifestation:* the physical embodiment of an *expression* of a *work*

▶ *Item:* a single exemplar of a *manifestation*

Work and *expression* are abstractions, whereas *manifestation* and *item* take physical form (or at least are embodied; for example, does an electronic file have a physical form?). In current cataloging practice, a manifestation is typically an abstract notion because it is the representation of a set of physical objects. In current bibliographic records only the most common characteristics shared by all *items* (copies) of a production or publication are represented. Even though Group 1 entities are presented in the model in the order of creation (from *work* to *item*), in actuality, it is typical that a library will start with the acquisition of an item and describe the *manifestation* in a bibliographic record. Very little information is currently recorded for the *expression* or *work* in either the bibliographic or authority records.

The four entities are linked together by relationships, as shown in Figure 2-1.

A *work* is realized through an *expression,* which in turn is embodied in a *manifestation,* which is exemplified by an *item.* This statement can also be reversed, since the relationships work both ways (an *item* exemplifies a *manifestation,* which embodies an *expression,* which in turn realizes a *work*). The relationships that exist between the Group 1 entities are also referred to as primary relationships. Notice that the links in Figure 2-1 have either single or double arrows. This indicates that one-to-many or many-to-many relationships exist between entities. This means, for example, that a *manifestation* can be exemplified by many *items* but an *item* can only exemplify one, not many, *manifestations.*

Often readers exposed to this terminology for the first time find it hard to grasp the interconnections of the four Group 1 entities.

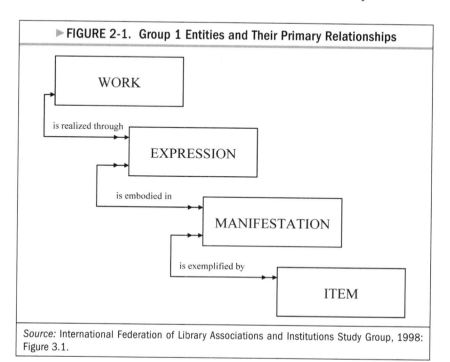

▶ **FIGURE 2-1. Group 1 Entities and Their Primary Relationships**

WORK

is realized through

EXPRESSION

is embodied in

MANIFESTATION

is exemplified by

ITEM

Source: International Federation of Library Associations and Institutions Study Group, 1998: Figure 3.1.

Let us look at an example that might help illustrate the entities and their relationships. An author has an idea for a story that involves a young orphan boy in England who is a wizard and ends up going to a wizardry and witchcraft school where he and his friends are involved in several adventures, and so on. This abstract story is a *work* resulting from a creative and intellectual endeavor. This story can be expressed (realized) in several possible ways. One of them is as a text in English, but it can also be expressed as a text in German or Greek or as a spoken performance (narration) in French or a number of other languages (see Figure 2-2). Each of these expressions can be manifested (embodied) in a variety of mediums and formats. In the example illustrated in Figure 2-2, the English textual expression has been embodied twice, once as a 1997 publication by Bloomsbury of London with the title *Harry Potter and the Philosopher's Stone* and once as a 1998 publication by Levine of New York with the title *Harry Potter and the Sorcerer's Stone.* Each of the other *expressions* of

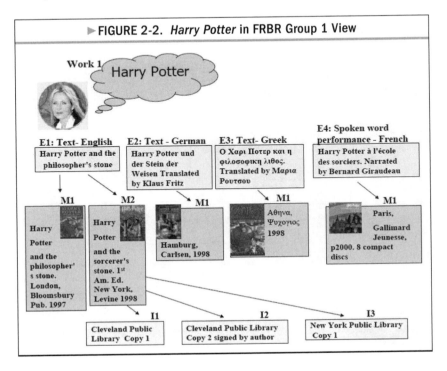

▶FIGURE 2-2. *Harry Potter* in FRBR Group 1 View

the same *work* has been embodied as at least one *manifestation*. The *manifestation* is a representation of the entire set of the particular publication or production. In other words, if the 1998 English publication by Levine includes one million copies, the *manifestation* represents the entire set of the one million copies. The individual copies on the other hand are the *items* that exemplify this particular *manifestation*.

Another way to illustrate the four entities using the above example (Figure 2-2) would be a bottom-up approach. The Cleveland Public Library, for example, has acquired a number of copies of *Harry Potter and the Sorcerer's Stone*, published by Levine in 1998, as has the New York Public Library. Each of these copies is considered a specific example of this particular publication; each is an *item* that exemplifies the entire set. The set of all of these items that share a number of common characteristics is the *manifestation*. The manifestation of the above example represents all copies of this particular publication. Based on current library standards for description and practice, each library creates a record describing the entire set, the *manifestation*, and not the individual copy, the *item*. This practice enables libraries to share records through copy cataloging. The particular manifestation often shares common characteristics with other manifestations, publications of the same story published as text in English but not necessarily by the same publisher. In other words, they all fall under the same *expression* (English text). There may be translations into other languages, other editions, or versions of the same content. These expressions are often indicated in current library records through the use of uniform titles, qualified by the language of the material. All of these expressions have a common story, common content that has not changed through the process of translation or expression in a different medium. This common story or content represents the *work*.

The second group of entities, labeled **Group 2,** represents the agents who are responsible for the intellectual or artistic content, the physical production and dissemination, or the custodianship of any Group 1 entity. The following Group 2 entities are included in the FRBR model:

▶ *Person:* an individual

▶ *Corporate body:* an organization or group of individuals and/or organizations

Relationships between any Group 2 entity and Group 1 entity and vice versa are identified in Figure 2-3.

A *work* is created by a *person* or a *corporate body,* an *expression* is realized by a *person* or a *corporate body,* a *manifestation* is produced

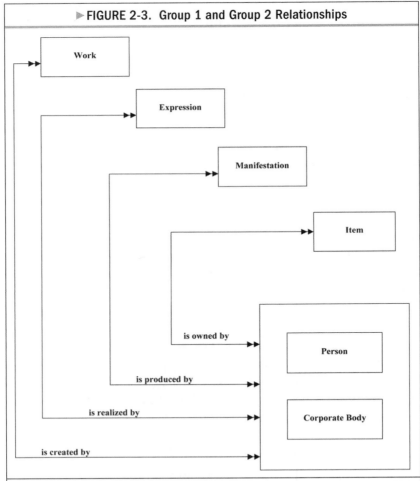

▶ FIGURE 2-3. Group 1 and Group 2 Relationships

Source: International Federation of Library Associations and Institutions Study Group, 1998: Figure 3.2.

by a *person* or a *corporate body*, and an *item* is owned by a *person* or a *corporate body*. Notice that all linking relationships in Figure 2-3 have double arrows, which means that the relationships are many-to-many. In this case, a *work* can be created by one or more Group 2 entities (*persons* or *corporate bodies*) and that a *person* or a *corporate body* can create one or more *works*.

Following the example in Figure 2-2, the *work, Harry Potter and the Sorcerer's Stone*, was created by a *person*, author J. K. Rowling, was realized as a German text by a *person*, translator Klaus Fritz, produced by a *corporate body*, publisher Levine, and is owned by *persons* and *corporate bodies*.

The third group of FRBR entities, **Group 3**, represents an additional set of entities that serve as the subjects of works. "Additional" here means that any Group 1 or Group 2 entity can serve as the subject of works but there are other entities, not defined in Groups 1 and 2, that can also serve as subjects. FRBR includes the following Group 3 entities:

▶ *Concept:* an abstract notion or idea

▶ *Object:* a material thing

▶ *Event:* an action or occurrence

▶ *Place:* a location

Only one relationship has been established between any Group 3 entity and the *work* entity from Group 1. The subject is associated in the model with a work because the subject does not change through the different expressions of the work or the different manifestations of each expression. In a particular implementation, it is possible to create work records and record the subjects at the work level that will then apply to any linked expression or manifestation records. This ensures consistency in subject representation and avoids unnecessary duplication of effort in performing subject analysis for all expressions and manifestations of a work (see Figure 2-4).

The *work* in Figure 2-2, *Harry Potter and the Sorcerer's Stone*, has as a subject the *concept* "wizards," the *place* "England," and so on. The subject does not change when the same work is expressed in a variety of ways (for example, translation into other languages), or

► FIGURE 2-4. FRBR Subject Relationship

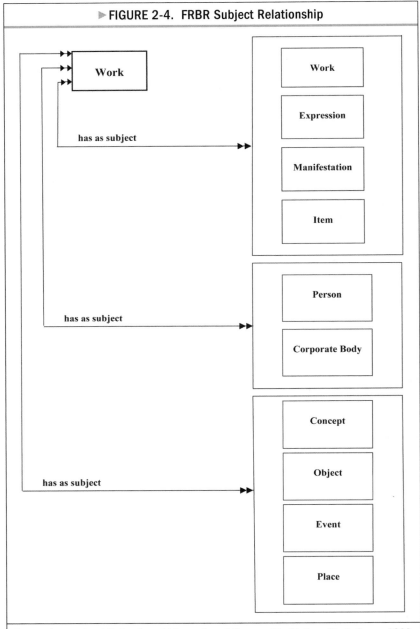

Source: International Federation of Library Associations and Institutions Study Group, 1998: Figure 3.3

when its expressions are embodied in different manifestations; neither is it different when comparing the subject of each of the items of the same manifestation.

In addition to the primary relationships between Group 1 entities and the basic relationships between Group 2 and 3 entities to Group 1 entities, FRBR identifies a number of other bibliographic relationships. These include relationships between works (such as supplements, parts, and adaptations), between expressions (such as translations, revisions, and musical arrangements), and between manifestations (such as simultaneous publications, production in different formats, and other reproductions).

In addition to the defined Group 1 entities, the model allows the flexibility of having both aggregate and component entities. For example, an anthology is an aggregate of several separate monographs, or a particular monograph can be a component entity of a publisher's series. In the FRBR model, both the aggregate and component entities function in the same way and have the same characteristics as the integral entities. Therefore, an aggregate work functions and has the same characteristics as an integral work.

For each of the Group 1, 2, and 3 entities, the model has identified the attributes, or main characteristics, by which these entities can be identified and described. There are two types of characteristics: those that are inherent in an entity and those that are externally attributed to an entity. Inherent attributes tend to be physical characteristics, observable attributes, whereas the externally attributed characteristics tend to be drawn from other sources such as vocabularies, identifier systems, etc. FRBR defines 12 attributes for *works*, 25 attributes for *expressions*, 38 attributes for *manifestations*, and 9 attributes for *items*. These attributes are not applicable to all works, expressions, manifestations, and items. For a particular work, only 5 of the 12 defined attributes may apply. Examples of *work* attributes include "title of the work" and "intended audience." Examples of *expression* attributes include "form of the expression" and "language of the expression." Examples of *manifestation* attributes include "place of publication" and "system requirements." Examples of *item* attributes include "item identifier" and "condition of item." A list of all identified attributes for

Group 1 entities and their definitions can be found in Chapter 4 of the *Functional Requirements for Bibliographic Records: Final Report* (International Federation of Library Associations and Institutions Study Group, 1998).

FRBR also identifies and defines attributes for Group 2 and 3 entities. Two working groups have been formed at IFLA that respectively cover these in more detail, and these will be discussed later in this chapter.

Entity attributes and relationships (the data) can be very useful to the end user performing search tasks in a catalog or other information retrieval system. These tasks are the reasons why a user might approach the catalog or use a bibliographic database to do research. FRBR defines these user tasks as the following (International Federation of Library Associations and Institutions Study Group, 1998: 8):

- ▶ Using the data to *find* materials that correspond to the user's stated search criteria (e.g., in the context of a search for all documents on a given subject or a search for a recording issued under a particular title)

- ▶ Using the data retrieved to *identify* an entity (e.g., to confirm that the document described in a record corresponds to the document sought by the user or to distinguish between two texts or recordings that have the same title)

- ▶ Using the data to *select* an entity that is appropriate to the user's needs (e.g., to select a text in a language the user understands or to choose a version of a computer program that is compatible with the hardware and operating system available to the user)

- ▶ Using the data in order to *acquire* or *obtain* access to the entity described (e.g., to place a purchase order for a publication, to submit a request for the loan of a copy of a book in a library's collection, or to access online an electronic document stored on a remote computer)

For example, a user might be trying to find a particular resource, the book *Harry Potter and the Sorcerer's Stone*, or a user might be looking for a book but not have a particular resource in mind (juvenile fiction that involves wizards). The user then needs to identify a particular expression of this resource (the text in English), and select a particular manifestation (the one published by Levine), and use the call number from the description of this manifestation to obtain/borrow a copy (the item). FRBR defines these user tasks as generic tasks performed by a user when searching for information. Each entity attribute and relationship is mapped to the user tasks it supports. A relative value (high, moderate, or low) of each attribute or relationship in supporting a specific user task is given for each of the four primary entities in the entity-relationship model. Tasks are further broken into four subtasks. For example, the user task *find* is broken into find a *work*, find an *expression*, find a *manifestation*, and find an *item*.

FURTHER DEVELOPMENT OF THE FRBR MODEL

The FRBR model is a conceptual model and thus open to different interpretations. Over the years, several issues and challenges have come to light. Thus, it is necessary to establish a mechanism for continuous review and revision. In 2003, the IFLA Cataloguing Section established the FRBR Review Group whose formal mandate includes the responsibility for making revisions to FRBR (International Federation of Library Associations and Institutions Functional Requirements for Bibliographic Records Review Group, 2008). Initially established as a working group in 2002, the Review Group is looking into several issues associated with the FRBR model, such as the expression entity, aggregate works, and harmonization with other conceptual models.

One of the areas needing further clarification was the definition of expression (Le Boeuf, 2005). As a response, the FRBR Review Group created the Working Group on The Expression Entity to clarify the interpretation of the expression entity that led to the first amendment proposal to the 1998 text of FRBR (International Federation of Library Associations and Institutions Working Group on the Expression Entity, 2007). The original text in the model states that any change in the content, no matter how minor it may be, is considered a change in *expression* and therefore results in a new *expression* (International Federation of Library Associations and Institutions Study Group, 1998). The Working Group on the Expression Entity proposed the revision of the text to read:

> ... if a text is revised or modified, the resulting *expression* is considered to be a new *expression*. Minor changes, such as corrections of spelling and punctuation, etc., are normally considered as variations within the same *expression*. However, for some applications of the model, each variation may be viewed as a different *expression*, such as variations between early texts of rare manuscripts. (International Federation of Library Associations and Institutions Working Group on Expression Entity, 2006: 2)

This revision eliminates the mandate to consider any minor change as a new expression and therefore a new record will not be required in such cases. Indeed, for the user, treating minor or insignificant changes in a text as the same expression may be less confusing than treating these changes as separate expressions. On the other hand, this revision means that some judgment will be required to determine when changes to a text become significant enough to constitute a new expression. This judgment can be left to individual catalogers or it might require going back to the practice of creating detailed rules to help catalogers decide when something is a new expression, something that had caused criticism of existing cataloging rules.

Although the model states that it covers all types of materials, it draws heavily from print monographs. Therefore, another important area needing further investigation is the modeling of aggregate works such as serials, series, collections and selections of works, and other whole/part cases. The Working Group on Aggregates, established in 2005, is focusing on these materials to provide a treatment equal to that which monographs had received in the original model (International Federation of Library Associations and Institutions Working Group on Aggregates, 2007).

A third group, the Working Group on FRBR/CRM Dialogue was created under the auspices of the FRBR Review Group to cooperate with the International Committee for Museum Documentation (CIDOC) Conceptual Reference Model (CRM) group in order to focus on interoperability between the FRBR and CRM models (International Federation of Library Associations and Institutions Working Group on Functional Requirements for Bibliographic Records/Conceptual Reference Model Dialogue, 2008). CIDOC CRM is a reference model and information standard that museums and other cultural heritage institutions can use to describe their collections and entities, with the ultimate goal of improving information sharing.

Three additional working groups were established but have since been disbanded. These include the Working Group on Continuing Resources, charged with investigating the model's coverage of continuing resources as well as assisting on revisions of the ISSN (International Standard Serial Number) standard; the Working Group on Subject Relationships, charged with a follow-up study to expand FRBR's and FRANAR's (Functional Requirements and Numbering of Authority Records) coverage of subject indexing and classification; and the Working Group on Teaching and Training, charged with the assessment of different methods for teaching FRBR to all types of audiences and the preparation of a manual for FRBR teachers.

THE FRBR MODEL FAMILY: FRAD AND FRSAD

FRBR covers bibliographic data, some of which are borrowed from authority data, such as access points. Additionally, the main focus of the FRBR model is on Group 1 entities. Two other IFLA working groups were established after the publication of the FRBR final report to focus on Group 2 and Group 3 entities respectively.

In April of 1999, the IFLA Division of Bibliographic Control, in conjunction with the IFLA Universal Bibliographic Control and International MARC Core Activity (UBCIM), established the Working Group on FRANAR to focus on Group 2 entities. The Working Group was charged with defining the functional requirements of authority data and with studying the feasibility of an international standard authority record number or numbering system. In 2005 the draft of the *Functional Requirements for Authority Records: A Conceptual Model* was released. After two worldwide reviews, the report titled *Functional Requirements for Authority Data: A Conceptual Model*, FRAD for short, was approved and published in June 2009 (International Federation of Library Associations and Institutions Working Group on Functional Requirements and Numbering of Authority Records, 2009).

FRAD has continued the work of FRBR, further identifying and defining attributes and relationships of Group 2 (and to some extent Group 3) entities with the addition of a number of new entities. FRAD is recommending the addition of *family* as a FRBR Group 2 entity after examining the need of the archival community to collocate collections based on families (Patton, 2007). *Family* is defined as "[t]wo or more persons related by birth, marriage, adoption, or similar legal status, or otherwise present themselves as a family" (International Federation of Library Associations and Institutions Working Group on the Functional Requirements and Numbering of Authority Records, 2007: 8). In addition, FRAD has defined *names* (characters or words by which an entity is known), *identifiers* (a number, code, etc. uniquely associated with an entity), *controlled access points* (the term, etc. by which a record can be found), *rules* (a set of instructions governing the formulation of a controlled access point), and *agencies* (the organization that creates and maintains controlled access points) as new entities required for authority data (International Federation of Library Associations and Institutions Working Group on the Functional Requirements and Numbering of Authority Records, 2007).

Authority data users include its creators as well as catalog users, who access authority data either directly (via authority files themselves) or indirectly (via controlled access points). Four general tasks have been defined in FRAD for these users:

▶ *Find* an entity or set of entities based on user criteria

▶ *Identify* an entity

▶ *Contextualize* or place an entity in context

▶ *Justify* the authority data creator's decision for a particular form of a name or controlled access point

Furthermore, in the same tradition as the FRBR model, FRAD defines entity attributes and relationships, mapping these to user tasks according to the value of importance for supporting each task. The Working Group is completing a new draft, which will be submitted for approval by the IFLA IV Division of Bibliographic Control.

In addition to the proposed FRAD model, the FRANAR Working Group released a paper that was approved by the Standing Committee of the IFLA Cataloguing Section in 2008. This paper includes an analysis of the feasibility of an International Standard Authority Data Number (ISADN) and recommendations for future actions.

The most recent IFLA working group to be established is the Working Group for the Functional Requirements for Subject Authority Records (FRSAR). The Working Group started in April of 2005, charged with building a conceptual model of Group 3 entities as they relate to the "aboutness" of works and with providing a clearly defined frame of reference for relating data recorded in authority records to the needs of subject authority data users (International Federation of Library Associations and Institutions Working Group on the Functional Requirements and Numbering of Authority Records, 2008). The first draft of the report was released for worldwide review in June 2009. *Functional Requirements for Subject Authority Data*, FRSAD for short, presents an abstract model for any FRBR entity used as a subject of a work, defining two entities, *thema* (any entity used as a subject of a work) and *nomen* (any sign or sequence of signs by which a thema is known, referred to or addressed), and a number of attributes and relationships (International Federation of Library Associations and Institutions Working Group on Functional Requirements for Subject Authority Records, 2009). Users of subject authority data are defined as information professionals such as metadata creators, reference librarians, controlled vocabulary creators, and end users who use information retrieval systems to fulfill their information needs (Salaba, Zeng, and Žumer, 2006). The Working Group has defined the following user tasks:

▶ *Find* a subject entity or set of entities that correspond to user's stated criteria

▶ *Identify* a subject entity based on specific attributes or characteristics

▶ *Select* an entity appropriate to a user's needs

▶ *Explore* relationships between entities (Žumer, Salaba, and Zeng, 2007)

It is hoped that once all three models are completed and approved they will be integrated, giving a complete picture of the bibliographic universe and modeling the functional requirements of bibliographic and authority data.

INTEROPERABILITY WITH OTHER MODELS

It is purported that the FRBR model covers all types of materials. Some discussions and reviews point out that the actual focus is primarily on textual monographic publications (Žumer, 2007). In order to be able to focus the discussion on and aid the applicability of the FRBR model with other communities such as archives, museums, and cultural heritage institutions, it is necessary to examine the feasibility of harmonizing the FRBR model with other conceptual models. To that end a new group, the FRBR/CRM Harmonization Group (a joint effort of IFLA and the International Council of Museums International Committee for Documentation [ICOM CIDOC]) was established. This group is working toward harmonizing FRBR with the ICOM CIDOC Conceptual Model (ICOM CIDOC CRM). Their objective is to produce an object-oriented version of FRBR (currently referred to as "FRBRoo") that would enrich the model with concepts deriving from the description of museum objects (Functional Requirements for Bibliographic Records/Conceptual Reference Model Dialogue, 2008). CRM is event-based, which brings an interesting perspective to further development of FRBR.

CRITICAL ISSUES AND CHALLENGES IN THE FRBR MODEL

Since the approval of the FRBR report in 1997 and its publication in 1998, there has been much speculation, discussion, and excitement about the prospects of implementing this model in library catalogs to benefit professionals and, more importantly, catalog users. But is the model complete and ready to be implemented?

Several issues have been raised about different components of the FRBR model and summaries of a select few are covered in this section. One of the most widely discussed issues is the definition of certain entities, particularly the entity *expression*. As discussed, IFLA responded to this issue by establishing the Working Group on the Expression Entity, which in turn developed the first amendment proposal to FRBR with a revised definition of what may constitute a change to content and, therefore, a change in expression. In the same line, the definition of *work*, a distinct intellectual or artistic creation, is also raising questions of what constitutes a new work. Are new editions with substantial content changes (especially for resources with a large number of editions) still the same work? How about very different performances of musical works? Should all variations, such as enlargements, abridgements, translations, adaptations for different audiences, or adaptations to different literary forms be considered different expressions of the same work or different works entirely? It appears as if the FRBR Working Group's decisions as to what constitutes a new work are often based on current description standards, namely the *Anglo-American Cataloguing Rules*, Second Edition (AACR2).

Another work-related issue is the often-cited need for the entity "superwork" (Smiraglia, 2007; Le Boeuf, 2002). The function of the superwork is mainly to serve as a collocating device designed to link related works such as all Hamlet works, including movies, performances, texts, and criticisms, many of which are separate works.

Additionally, some of the issues relate to the attributes for each Group 1 entity as defined in FRBR. For example, the attribute "title of work" assumes the use of the current "uniform title," often governed by a particular description standard (typically AACR2 biased). The same is true for the attribute "title of expression." It is interesting to note that these two attributes do not exist in FRAD, which defines the entity *name* instead, where the title is a possible value for the attribute *name*. "Date of work" is used for the creation date, which often is not easy to find or decide on. For example, if a person started creating a work in 2004, finished the manuscript and submitted it for publication in 2006, and was finally published in 2008, how often are all these dates publically available and which date is the "date of work"? The same issue exists with the expression attribute "date of expression."

There are also cases where there is a question of whether or not a piece of information is an entity attribute or a relationship between entities. For example, FRBR defines "statement of responsibility" as a manifestation attribute (based on AACR2), which begs the question, is a statement of responsibility an attribute of a manifestation or is it a relationship between a *work, expression,* or *manifestation* and a *person* or a *corporate body?* Is the "place of publication" an attribute of a manifestation or a relationship between a manifestation and the entity *place?* A more extensive discussion of all FRBR entity attributes and some issues involved with each of them is covered by Maxwell (2008).

In an effort to gain a better understanding of what needs to be done in the immediate future, expert participants in a Delphi Study were asked to identify critical issues in the areas of the FRBR model, evaluation, modification, and its relation to other models, and to also rate the importance of these issues (Zhang and Salaba, 2009). The FRBR model was the area with the most issues raised among all areas included in the study. Verification and validation of the model using real data were considered keys to future acceptance, development, and modification of the model and received the highest rating among all issues identified. Model validation will help us develop or modify standards of description that integrate the model. Another issue raised is the necessity of examining the model's applicability to different environments and types of materials (discussed in more detail in Chapter 4). Finally, another of the critical issues most highly ranked was testing the model's validity with real user studies to better understand the benefits of a FRBR-based catalog to end users.

The FRBR model is still evolving and several issues need to be addressed for a more meaningful and successful implementation. Chapter 3 discusses how the acceptance of the FRBR model may influence and transform our description standards and cataloging and metadata practices currently and in the near future.

REFERENCES

International Federation of Library Associations and Institutions Functional Requirements for Bibliographic Records Review Group. 2008. "FRBR Review Group." Available: www.ifla.org/en/frbr-rg (accessed July 30, 2009).

International Federation of Library Associations and Institutions Study Group on the Functional Requirements for Bibliographic Records. 1998. *Functional Requirements for Bibliographic Records: Final Report.* Munich, Germany: K. G. Saur.

International Federation of Library Associations and Institutions Working Group on Aggregates. 2007. "Working Group on Aggregates." Available: www.ifla .org/en/node/923 (accessed July 30, 2009).

International Federation of Library Associations and Institutions Working Group on the Expression Entity. 2006. "FRBR Chapter 3: Entities: Proposed Changes to the FRBR Text." Available: www.frbr.org/files/FRBR-expression-2006-marked-up.pdf (accessed July 30, 2009).

International Federation of Library Associations and Institutions Working Group on the Expression Entity. 2007. "Working Group on the Expression Entity." Available: www.ifla.org/files/cataloguing/frbrrg/expression-wg-activities_2006-2007.pdf (accessed July 30, 2009).

International Federation of Library Associations and Institutions Working Group on Functional Requirements for Bibliographic Records/Conceptual Reference Model Dialogue. 2008. "Working Group on FRBR/CRM Dialogue." Available: www.ifla.org/en/node/928 (accessed July 30, 2009).

International Federation of Library Associations and Institutions Working Group on the Functional Requirements and Numbering of Authority Records. 2007. "Functional Requirements for Authority Data: A Conceptual Model. 2nd Draft." Available: www.ifla.org/en/publications/ifla-series-on-bibliographic-control-34 (accessed July 30, 2009).

International Federation of Library Associations and Institutions Working Group on the Functional Requirements for Subject Authority Records. 2008. [Homepage]. Available from www.ifla.org/en/node/1296 (accessed July 30, 2009).

International Federation of Library Associations and Institutions Working Group on Functional Requirements. 2009. *Functional Requirements for Subject Authority Data (FRSAD).* Draft report. Available: www.ifla .org/en/node/1297 (accessed July 20, 2009).

International Federation of Library Associations and Institutions Working Group on Functional Requirements and Numbering of Authority Records (FRANAR). 2009. *Functional Requirements for Authority Data: A Conceptual Model,* edited by Glenn E. Patton. München: K.G. Sauer.

Le Boeuf, Patrick. 2002. "The Impact of the FRBR Model on the Future Revisions of the ISBDs: A Challenge for the IFLA Section on Cataloguing." *International Cataloguing and Bibliographic Control: Quarterly Bulletin of the IFLA UBCIM Programme* 31, no. 1: 3–6.

Le Boeuf, Patrick. 2005. "FRBR: Hype or Cure-all? Introduction." *Cataloging & Classification Quarterly* 39, no. 3/4: 1–13.

Madison, Olivia M. A. 2005. "The Origins of the IFLA Study on Functional Requirements for Bibliographic Records." *Cataloging & Classification Quarterly* 39, no. 3/4: 15–37.

Maxwell, Robert L. 2008. *FRBR: A Guide for the Perplexed.* Chicago: American Library Association.

Patton, Glenn E. 2007. "Understanding the Relationship between FRBR and FRAD." In *Understanding FRBR: What It Is and How It Will Affect Our Retrieval Tools* (pp. 2–34), edited by Arlene G. Taylor. Westport, CT: Libraries Unlimited.

Salaba, Athena, Marcia L. Zeng, and Maja Žumer. 2006. "Functional Requirements for Subject Authority Records." In *Knowledge Organization for a Global Learning Society: Proceedings of the Ninth International ISKO Conference, 4–7 July 2006, Vienna, Austria* (pp. 101–106), edited by Gerhard Budin, Christian Swerz, and Konstantin Mitgutsch. Würzburg: Ergon Verlag.

Smiraglia, Richard P. 2007. "Bibliographic Families and Superworks." In *Understanding FRBR: What It Is and How It Will Affect Our Retrieval Tools* (pp. 73–86), edited by Arlene G. Taylor. Westport, CT: Libraries Unlimited.

Zhang, Yin, and Athena Salaba. 2009. "What Is Next for FRBR? A Delphi Study." *The Library Quarterly* 79, no. 2: 233–255.

Žumer, Maja. 2007. "FRBR: The End of the Road or a New Beginning." *Bulletin of the American Society for Information Science and Technology* 33, no. 6: 27–29.

Žumer, Maja, Athena Salaba, and Marcia Zeng. 2007. "Functional Requirements for Subject Authority Records (FRSAR): A Conceptual Model of Aboutness." *Asian Digital Libraries: Looking Back 10 Years and Forging New Frontiers. Proceedings of the 10th International Conference on Asian Digital Libraries (ICADL 2007), 10–13 December 2007, Hanoi, Vietnam.* Publication appears in *Lecture Notes in Computer Science (LNCS).*

IMPACT OF FRBR ON CURRENT CATALOGING STANDARDS AND PRACTICE

A s discussed in Chapter 2, FRBR (Functional Requirements for Bibliographic Records) is a conceptual model of the bibliographic universe specifying entities and their attributes as well as the relationships between entities. In addition, FRBR attempts to tie user tasks to a number of entity attributes, thus indicating the value of these attributes in supporting a specific user task. In other words, these associations could be used to generate a list of attributes that should be mandatory for a bibliographic description in order to support a number of fundamental catalog functions. Attributes could be further divided into those attributes that are either desirable or support secondary functions and attributes that are optional. For example, according to FRBR, the attribute of highest value in finding a work is the "title of the work," whereas the "form of the work" is of medium value and the "date of the work" is of low value for the finding task.

Catalogs and the information they store, mainly bibliographic records, should be designed to support the functions of a catalog, which are defined by the user tasks. The revisions of existing description standards to incorporate FRBR elements or to support the development of new FRBR-based resource description standards is necessary in order to ensure viable description of and access to bibliographic resources.

WHAT CHANGES WILL FRBR BRING?

It is hoped that the implementation of FRBR will lead to the development of standards for creating uniform metadata that facilitate interoperability and, therefore, will allow bibliographic information to be shared not only among all libraries in the world but also between all information agencies, such as museums, digital libraries, and archives. The need for such metadata, driven by the FRBR model, requires several changes in the area of metadata creation, including new or revised standards for description and access, new or revised encoding standards, a restructuring of bibliographic and authority records, and the reuse of existing metadata.

Tillett gives an overview of the way FRBR might be applied to international cataloging principles, cataloging rules, or standards of description to construct future catalogs that better identify and collocate related bibliographic entities (Tillett, 2005). This could be done by using existing bibliographic and authority data and building on our existing data and practices to create new record structures to facilitate increased interoperability and accessibility. This would expand the possibilities for end users for finding the information they want.

Changes in current cataloging principles and standards, development of new standards, and some possibilities for additional necessary changes are covered in the following sections. In addition, suggested changes to current practices and the ways in which cataloging in general might be changing in light of FRBR implementation are discussed.

INTERNATIONAL CATALOGUING PRINCIPLES

The "Paris Principles," the first international cataloging principles, were the result of the first international conference of cataloging experts sponsored by IFLA (International Federation of Library Associations and Institutions) in Paris, France in 1961 (International Conference on Cataloguing Principles, 1963). Since that time, these principles have been providing the foundation for the development of all contemporary cataloging standards.

Starting in 2003, IFLA began reexamining of the Paris Principles to ensure they reflected the current cataloging environments and to expand them to include both descriptive and subject cataloging in an effort to adapt the principles. There were five IFLA Meetings of Experts on an International Cataloguing Code (IME ICC) between 2003 and 2007 and, after each meeting, draft statements were made available for review. The revised principles (the final draft, April 10, 2008, was available for worldwide review until June 30, 2008) built on cataloging traditions from around the world as well as on newer conceptual models, namely IFLA's FRBR and FRAD (Functional Requirements for Authority Data) models. The document states that it "is hoped these principles will increase the international sharing of bibliographic and authority data and guide cataloguing rule makers in their efforts to develop an international cataloguing code" (International Federation of Library Associations and Institutions Meeting of Experts on an International Cataloguing Code, 2008: 1). The statement incorporates FRBR concepts such as the entities in bibliographic records (work, expression, manifestation, and item) and all Group 1, 2, and 3 entities, as defined in FRBR, as well as entities in authority records, entity attributes, and entity relationships. The FRBR model is also reflected in the way in which the draft statement describes the functions of a catalog: to "find" (further specified as to "locate" based on Svenonius, 2000), "identify," and "select" bibliographic resources, to "acquire" or "obtain" access to an item or a record, and to "navigate" the catalog and beyond.

The revision of the *International Cataloguing Principles* to reflect the FRBR model suggests the need for revising cataloging standards to include rules that meet with worldwide acceptance and that rigorously consider the user tasks of culturally different user groups.

DESCRIPTION STANDARDS

International Standard Bibliographic Description

In order to assure consistency between bibliographic standards, IFLA reconstituted the International Standard Bibliographic Description (ISBD) Review Group to work on a full review of the

ISBDs. An initial task of the Review Group was to align the terminology used in the ISBDs with that used in FRBR. This alignment proved to be challenging, mainly because FRBR is an abstract, high-level conceptual model and ISBD includes specifications at a much more detailed level. Therefore, one of the objectives of this review became to ensure conformity between the provisions of the ISBDs and the FRBR data requirements for the basic-level national bibliographic record (International Federation of Library Associations and Institutions International Standard Bibliographic Description Review Group, 2008). As a result, Tom Delsey developed a mapping between ISBD elements and FRBR attributes and relationships in 2004 (International Federation of Library Associations and Institutions International Standard Bibliographic Description Review Group, 2004). This mapping required the examination of ISBD elements and the assurance that all mapped optional FRBR attributes also became optional elements in the ISBDs so that no mandatory FRBR element was aligned with an optional ISBD element. A number of changes were suggested for the ISBDs. Despite these changes, however, the main structure and elements of the ISBDs "have proved relatively stable over the years and continue to be widely used in full or part by creators of cataloguing codes and metadata schemes" (International Federation of Library Associations and Institutions International Standard Bibliographic Description Review Group, 2008).

A new project was started in 2003 to consolidate all specialized ISBDs into a single document. The primary publication of this consolidation was published in 2007[1] and its first update is expected in 2009.

Resource Description and Access

The major cataloging standard used in most Anglo-American libraries, and many other libraries in the world that follow their practices, is the *Anglo-American Cataloguing Rules* (AACR). Since its second edition, AACR has been slowly revised. Still, there was such a call for fundamental revision that it led to the International Conference on the Principles & Future Development of AACR, sponsored by the Joint Steering Committee for Revision of AACR

(JSC). Fifty-three experts presented nine papers at this conference, which took place in Toronto, Canada in October of 1997[2] (Joint Steering Committee for the Development of Resource Description and Access, 2009). These papers covered issues relating to the nature of a work, access points for works, bibliographic relationships, seriality, and modeling AACR. A number of actions were taken between 1997 and 2005. One of these actions was to revise rule 0.24 to address the description of expressions of a work and the variations among their manifestations. JSC charged the international Format Variation Working Group (FVWG) with testing the practicality of creating expression-level records. This, of course, was in alignment with FRBR and its concept of expression. The group was disbanded (or discharged in IFLA's terms) in 2004 after the report on their work on AACR Chapter 25 to include rules for creating expression headings, general material designators (GMDs), and their failed effort to create an experimental database. FVWG suggested that cataloging at the level of expression might be difficult for most libraries and that expression-based collocation might be more helpful than expression-level cataloging (Bowen, 2005).

The initial work on revising AACR was titled "AACR3: Resource Description and Access," and a draft of Part I of AACR3 was made available for review in December 2004. It was at this stage in 2005 that JSC decided to change the title to "RDA: Resource Description and Access." The new document, RDA (Resource Description and Access), defined its scope and structure in relation to conceptual models, both the ones on which it is based and other metadata models. RDA incorporates terminology and concepts from FRBR and FRAD, particularly in the way it covers descriptive data and access based on these data, and it is developed in accordance with the IME ICC Statement of International Cataloguing Principles.

RDA is intended to cover rules for descriptive metadata (for both resources and content), regardless of whether they will be stored in bibliographic records, authority records, or some other record structure (Tillett, 2007b). Drafts of various RDA parts have been made available for review since December 2005. In addition to the RDA standard, three supplementary documents have been created: "RDA Element Analysis," "RDA to FRBR Mapping," and "RDA to FRAD Mapping." The release of the new standards has been postponed a few times, and it is now scheduled for release in November of 2009. After its release, several national libraries plan to evaluate RDA before they decide if they will implement it.

RDA faces a number of criticisms; Coyle and Hillmann (2007) summarized some of these issues:

► RDA is based on FRBR and both are placing emphasis on bibliographic description. Users spend less time with bibliographic description and more time browsing electronic texts and interactive resources.

► In the RDA prospectus it is stated that data produced using RDA need to be integrated into existing files, which are limited to data produced using AACR2 and MARC formats.

► RDA's focus is still on the "resource," which aligns to FRBR's manifestation and item descriptions but with only some of the elements of works and expressions.

► RDA contains a number of legacy approaches, such as the use of "primary" and "secondary" notions, creating textual "uniform titles," and identifying relationships between works with the use of textual citation-like notes instead of linking devices such as Uniform Resource Identifiers (URIs).

► RDA's goals include one of "ease and efficiency of use," but the detailed rules included in RDA are comparable in number and complexity to AACR2.

► RDA is trying to appeal to other environments and not just the traditional library environment of AACR2, but it might not be flexible enough for simpler or less-structured approaches to description and computer mediation to provide user services.

Overall, the criticism is that RDA might be following the complexity and conventions of AACR2 too closely and has not provided evidence for new ways of dealing with bibliographic descriptions that would be applicable to a larger variety of information environments.

Criticism of RDA is also evident in the lack of support by the library community. ALA's Committee on Cataloging: Description and Access (CC:DA) suggested that RDA adopt a "top-down" approach. According to this approach, RDA should provide a set of principled general rules and then assess the need and appropriateness of more specific rules. The CC:DA also recommended that RDA be reviewed as a whole and not just as separate parts and, therefore, that its timeline be revised. Lastly, the CC:DA suggested that RDA should use other description standards, models, and ideas such as DACS (Department of Defense Information Analysis Center), Dublin Core (DC), and CCO (Cataloging Cultural Objects) (American Library Association Committee on Cataloging: Description and Access, 2006). Thus far, RDA has included mappings to ISBD, MARC, and DC as appendixes. In addition, the Library of Congress, the National Library of Medicine, and the National Agricultural Library in the United States made a joint decision to continue supporting the development of RDA and to complete the development of RDA, but they also plan to "conduct appropriate tests that will inform and involve the broader U.S. library community as to the utility of the code, and to ensure a product that is useful, usable, and cost effective" before a decision is made as to whether to implement RDA (Library of Congress, National Library of Medicine, and National Agricultural Library, 2008: 3). The conclusion of this testing is not anticipated before 2010, at the earliest. This announcement by the three national libraries to delay the decision for RDA implementation has contributed to community uncertainty toward RDA implementation.

Even though RDA is based on standards that come out of the Anglo-American cataloging tradition, it is being developed as an international standard to be used by any country and for any information environment. The international community has joined in providing comments and suggestions during the review process. Among the involved parties are the Deutsche Nationalbibliothek, the Svensk Biblioteksförenings kommitté för katalogisering (The Cataloguing Committee of the Swedish Library Association), the National Library of Sweden, the Australian Committee on Cataloguing (an RDA joint author), and the British Library.

Dublin Core Metadata Initiative

At a meeting to discuss the fit between RDA and models used in other metadata communities held at the British Library on April 30 and May 1, 2007, it was announced that the RDA and DC communities would work together to develop a formal RDA Element Vocabulary (a registry of RDA elements readable both by humans and machine); to develop an RDA/DC application profile based on the DC Abstract Model (DCAM), FRBR, and FRAD; and to use RDF and SKOS (Simple Knowledge Organization System) to disclose RDA value vocabularies. The benefits of such an endeavor are that the library environment will develop a metadata standard compatible and interoperable with the Semantic Web initiatives; the Dublin Core Metadata Initiative (DCMI) will have a library application profile based on models such as DCAM and FRBR, to serve as an example of a high-level profile for other communities; the Semantic Web will have a good set of metadata terms; and RDA will receive wider acceptance (Dublin Core Metadata Initiative/Resource Description and Access Task Group, 2008; British Library, 2007). As of this writing, an RDA registry sandbox for a number of RDA vocabularies is available at http://metadataregistry.org.

Other Cataloging Standards

One of the cataloging standards groups to consider incorporating FRBR early on was the RICA Standing Commission. RICA—Regole italiane di catalogazione per autori (Italian Cataloging Rules for Authors)—is a national set of requirements for the choice of authors based on the Paris Principles and ISBD. As of 2002, the RICA Standing Committee began the process of revising its rules to incorporate the FRBR model. According to the Standing Commission, FRBR represents the "most complete and logical frame of relevance to be found today, and the one according to which the revisions of Italian cataloguing rules should be developed" (Regole italiane di catalogazione per autori Standing Commission, 2002: 29). However, the Commission deemed that closer examination, verification, and discussion were necessary in the library community due to a number of issues that needed practical solutions. Since then, the new Italian cataloging rules have been presented and are available on the Web (Commissione Regole italiane di catalogazione per autori, 2009).

CHANGES IN ENCODING STANDARDS

The majority of current library records are encoded using MARC (MARC21, UNIMARC, or another MARC-based standard). MARC serves both as an exchange format and also as a logical model of bibliographic data. It is one of the richest metadata formats because of its ability to express detailed bibliographic information. On the other hand, it is domain specific (used mainly by libraries and not by other environments such as digital libraries, museums, etc.) and not all software supports it.

MARC might be considered an "old-fashioned" format, but because of its wide use for current bibliographic data it will be around for a while. With the development of FRBR and the various projects to develop or revise cataloging standards to handle attributes, relationships, and elements defined in FRBR and to support user tasks, one may ask two questions relating to MARC:

▶ Are the existing MARC formats able to express FRBR elements and structures?

▶ Is MARC in the future of FRBR-based catalog records or should we adopt or develop a different schema?

Existing MARC Records

Through an analysis of MARC data, Hegna and Murtomaa (2003) examined whether FRBR elements could be found in existing MARC records and, if so, how these MARC elements could be used for FRBR displays in a library catalog (or in a FRBR interface). Their analysis shows that even though the current records hold information on attributes relevant to identifying the work, expression, and manifestation entities, the accuracy and formal syntax are too simple to be properly handled by the systems. Some fields could be tied to a FRBR entity, but there was not enough information (or sometimes the information was incorrect) to determine to which entity this information belonged.

The FVWG also examined MARC21 elements that would allow expression-level cataloging as well as how feasible it would be for MARC records to handle multiple formats (Joint Steering Committee for the Revision of AACR, Format Variation Working Group, 2002). Their findings state that:

- ▶ although the FRBR entities manifestation and item are concrete, works and expressions can often be discovered only by comparing similar manifestations; and

- ▶ based on Delsey's functional analysis of MARC bibliographic and holdings fields (Network Development and MARC Standards Office, 2006), of the 30 expression-level attributes defined in FRBR, half of them have no specific MARC21 tag to contain them. Additional expression-level attributes are often included in nonspecific notes fields.

The group concluded that "while thinking about cataloging at the expression-level may be intuitive for catalogers in some specific settings (such as archives), it is neither logical nor practical as a starting point for most library cataloging" (Joint Steering Committee for the Revision of AACR, Format Variation Working Group, 2002). Instead of creating expression-level records, the group suggested accommodating expression-level collocation. For this purpose, the group started considering how best to display relationships between records in an intelligible way. A number of possible approaches to show variations using MARC records are discussed later in this chapter.

MARC Encoding in the Future of FRBR-based Records

Aalberg presented data based on the FRBRization experiments of the Norwegian BIBSYS database showing how MARC might or might not support FRBR (Aalberg, 2007). He suggested that current MARC formats can express very basic FRBR scenarios such as a single person having created a work, which is realized through an expression, then embodied in a manifestation, and finally exemplified as an item. It becomes more complicated when there is a need to express other scenarios, such as when one work or expression is linked to many occurrences of Group 2 entities (many persons created or realized it), when many works are embodied in one manifestation, and especially when one manifestation embodies many works, each of them linked to many Group 2 entities. He pointed to many issues with existing MARC records (missing information, inadequate linking of entities, inconsistent practices, etc.) and how it is not always clear which entities the different MARC elements represent (uniform titles for works and expression, expression information in various codes and subfields, etc.). Aalberg concluded that MARC is a rich format that allows for very detailed bibliographic information and is surprisingly expressive when it is used to its full extent. However, it is not as flexible and generic as XML (eXtensible Markup Language). His answer to the question of whether MARC is the right solution for the future is twofold. Considering the existing legacy data, his answer is yes, MARC will still be the solution; considering future records without worrying about compatibility with legacy data, his answer is that XML-based structures are the solution (Aalberg, 2007).

Tillett has presented many works on RDA and the related standards and efforts. Among them is the mapping of RDA elements to MARC21 (Tillett, 2007a). This was deemed necessary since the majority of U.S. libraries are using MARC and will most likely continue using MARC21 for RDA records. A mapping of elements between RDA and MARC21 is also included in RDA's appendixes in addition to a mapping of elements to Dublin Core. According to Tillett, it is expected that existing MARC21 structures will be able to incorporate most RDA data, and in most cases, RDA will not require changes to MARC21.

It seems that the future of RDA and MARC in relation to FRBR implementation is a complex one. Some believe that MARC and RDA will serve the purposes of FRBR and others believe that both will need extensive revisions in order to accommodate FRBR-based descriptions. MARC is considered a flat structure, and FRBR's need to express detailed and often complex relationships among entities might require a different structure.

ONIX

ONIX, developed by EDItEUR, is an international standard for presenting publishing industry product information in an electronic format. ONIX records include descriptive metadata, among others, that can be shared and used in both library and publishing environments. In April 2006, JSC (responsible for RDA) and EDItEUR (responsible for ONIX) formed a joint initiative, supported by the British Library, to develop a framework for categorizing resources in all media. This framework will support the needs of libraries and the publishing industry and will facilitate sharing of resource descriptions between these environments (RDA/ONIX Initiative, 2008).

Drawing from the RDA/ONIX framework and previous recommendations by the GMD/SMD (Standard Material Designation) Working Group, three new data elements—Media type, Carrier type, and Content type—have been proposed for RDA. These elements are designed to assist users in fulfilling the *select* user tasks of FRBR.

Resource Description Framework Schema

The Resource Description Framework (RDF) is a set of W3C specifications for describing resources and stating relationships between entities (called resources in RDF). These relationships are expressed as a set of statements using triplets (in the form of subject, predicate, object). One important concept for RDF is the use of URIs for identification of resources on the Web. Properties in an RDF schema are always expressed as URI references. There are a number of discussions and efforts to examine how RDF can be used for bibliographic data. One such effort by Styles, Ayers, and Shabir (2008) was presented at the Linked Data on the Web conference (LDOW 2008) on the feasibility of transforming MARC21 data into RDF. In their paper they also discuss the representation of FRBR-based data using RDF, a topic based on Davis and Newman's (2005) RDF expression of the FRBR model.

At the same time, there is an effort by the FRBR community to explore the representation of FRBR in RDF and to set up a schema and a namespace. This work, started by Gordon Dunsire, is currently available through the NSDL's (National Science Digital Library) metadata registry sandbox. Vocabularies in the register include FRBR Entities, FRBR Relationships, FRBR Relationships as concepts, and FRBR User Tasks.[3] The FRBR Review Group agreed that an authoritative FRBR namespace in RDF is necessary and that it is appropriate to carry out under the auspices of the FRBR Review Group. Their task was "*To define appropriate* namespaces for FRBR (entity-relationship) in RDF and other appropriate syntaxes" (International Federation of Library Associations and Institutions Functional Requirements for Bibliographic Records Review Group, 2007: 4). In the 2008 report to the FRBR Review Group, Dunsire (International Federation of Library Associations and Institutions Functional Requirements for Bibliographic Records Review Group, 2008: 1–2) states, "A major impetus behind the project was the formation of the DCMI RDA Task Group. This group aims to define components of *RDA: Resource Description and Access* as an RDF vocabulary for use in developing a Dublin Core application profile. RDA is based on FRBR, and RDA metadata attributes are mapped to FRBR entities." The Review Group decided that the development of FRBR namespace should build on the work by the DCMI/RDA Task Group and continue to use the NSDL Metadata Registry.

This effort is a welcomed advancement toward the Semantic Web and the creation of a formal and authoritative vocabulary that will allow FRBR implementation on the Web and beyond the traditional library environment.

ARE CHANGES IN CATALOGING PRACTICE COMING SOON?

Our information environment has changed and is constantly changing. More information is available in a larger variety of formats and new venues (such as the Internet) and is created and produced by both the traditional publishing industry and nontraditional environments. While our library catalogs were once viewed as a valuable means for finding, storing, and sharing information, our users no longer see the library catalog as the only source for locating information, published or otherwise. Often they do not see it as the first or the easiest tool to use. The tradition of describing resources by information professionals using detailed standards is not the only way to create resource description anymore. Other environments offer resource descriptions; therefore, the sharing of information between environments needs to be more flexible. We need simpler standards to be able to support the description of new forms of intellectual output, to reuse existing data, and to efficiently describe new materials (Coyle and Hillman, 2007).

Our current cataloging rules, AACR2 and the proposed RDA, have been faced with the criticism of not being flexible or interoperable with other metadata standards. Even RDA, which has been redesigned to incorporate FRBR, is still criticized for placing the main focus on the description of manifestations and items, as AACR2 does. Cataloging standards need to be flexible enough to support not only human-created metadata but also machine-generated metadata.

Because RDA is still under development and there is lingering uncertainty as to when and how it might be implemented, the cataloging community is anxiously waiting to see what the future holds for cataloging. It has been proposed that the impact of RDA on current records will be minimal, and it will not be costly to implement it.

Others have experimented with working to convert our current records into FRBR-based structures, but without standards and a clear and common understanding of what FRBR-based record structures are, a variety of scenarios have been proposed. Vendors have been experimenting with new record structures and the redisplay of existing record information into FRBR displays.

Current record structures are based on AACR2 and MARC implementations. Three types of records are created using MARC: bibliographic records, containing mainly *manifestation* information; authority records, containing Group 2 entity information (either as creators of Group 1 entities or of subjects of works), subjects, and *work/expression* information; and holdings records, containing *item* information. Since this information is based on AACR2, it is not always as complete as in FRBR.

In a 2005 report to the Machine-Readable Bibliographic Information (MARBI) Committee, Sally McCallum of the Library of Congress proposed two models for FRBR-based record structures (McCallum, 2005). In the first model, Model A, it is proposed that work and expression information be contained in authority records, manifestation information in bibliographic records, and item information in holdings records. Information about subjects and Group 2 entities (both as creators but also as producers, editors, etc.) would also be contained in authority records. Authority information would be linked to and from bibliographic records as illustrated in Figure 3-1.

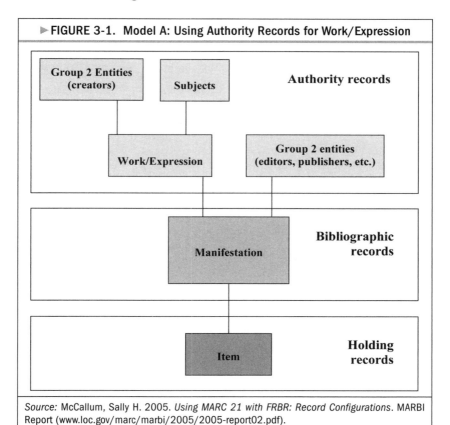

▶ FIGURE 3-1. Model A: Using Authority Records for Work/Expression

Source: McCallum, Sally H. 2005. *Using MARC 21 with FRBR: Record Configurations*. MARBI Report (www.loc.gov/marc/marbi/2005/2005-report02.pdf).

Notice that there are links between authority records and authority and manifestation records. When creating an authority record for a work/expression, linked information on creators and others responsible for a work or an expression is used directly from Group 2 authority records, as is subject information, since the subject relationship exists between subjects and works only. Other authority information (such as a Group 2 entity acting as a publisher) is directly linked to manifestation/bibliographic records.

The second model, Model B, proposes the use of bibliographic records for work/expression information. The structure and links between records in Model B are illustrated in Figure 3-2.

McCallum continues with a table of elements needed for work/expression records, whether they are located in current bibliographic or authority records and whether they are missing from current records.

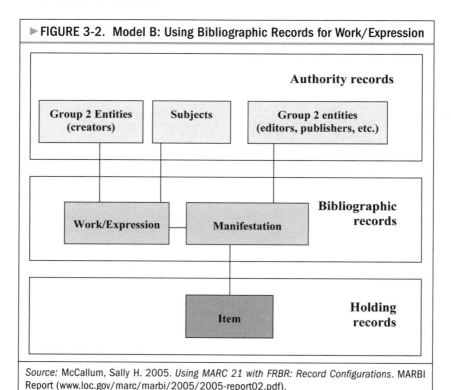

▶ FIGURE 3-2. Model B: Using Bibliographic Records for Work/Expression

Source: McCallum, Sally H. 2005. *Using MARC 21 with FRBR: Record Configurations.* MARBI Report (www.loc.gov/marc/marbi/2005/2005-report02.pdf).

Taking into consideration the McCallum report and the currently developed RDA, MARBI proposed that even though there are a number of FRBR implementations using existing MARC data to create user displays, "it is believed that explicit coding in bibliographic and authority records to identify works and expressions will help to facilitate more effective displays and support for user tasks" (Resource Description and Access/MARC Working Group, 2008). In this report, three scenarios are described and illustrated with examples. These scenarios include:

- ▶ works and expressions as authority records, manifestations as bibliographic records;
- ▶ works, expressions, and manifestations as bibliographic records; and
- ▶ manifestations that do not need independent work or expression records.

Based on these scenarios, MARBI proposed the addition of a new MARC field (011), which defines whether a record is for a work or an expression, with an option to indicate whether it is for a manifestation.

Parallel scenarios include consideration of whether it would be more beneficial to continue with manifestation-level cataloging, to move to expression-level cataloging, or to take a single-record approach. These discussions are typically related to serial cataloging and multiple versions or format variations and therefore will be discussed in Chapter 4 under application for Serials, Other Continuing Resources, and Aggregates.

Cataloging with FRBR is easier because the work and expressions will need to be described only once. The system can take advantage of the FRBR structure and automatically link or repeat the information that is inherited from the higher levels of work and expression to manifestation and item. Current practice, which is based on cataloging manifestations, requires the repetition of work and expression information every time a new manifestation is described.

Authority files are very important to cataloging and contribute, or have a great potential to contribute, in the precision of searching library catalogs and the Web. With FRBR, authority records and the ability to share authority records among different environments throughout the world is becoming more important than before. It is very important to be able to identify works and expressions, which is done through the use of uniform titles (and will continue to be done this way if RDA is implemented). Another change in our cataloging practice is to make sure we not only create the appropriate and necessary authority records but also use the work identifiers in expression and manifestation records and the expression identifiers in manifestation records. An examination of current MARC records that represent manifestations shows that cataloging practice for whether a uniform title authority record is created is inconsistent and that many manifestation records that are variations (and therefore under authority control) are missing uniform titles or other linking elements (Zhang and Salaba, 2009a).

A great contribution to authority files and of great importance to standardized vocabularies worldwide is the Virtual International Authority File (VIAF). VIAF (www.oclc.org/research/projects/viaf) is virtual because it builds on existing authority files by linking to existing national and regional authority files. VIAF allows users to bring together all authority information about an entity from many countries and in many languages and enables the user to select their preferred display. With FRBR in place and its companions FRAD and the RDA, under development as an international standard of description, and with VIAF under way, it looks like the path is laid for international cataloging standards and practice.

CRITICAL ISSUES AND CHALLENGES IN CATALOGING STANDARDS AND PRACTICE

The need for internationally agreed upon cataloging standards is made evident by the outcome of the Delphi Study with a group of FRBR experts (Zhang and Salaba, 2009b). "Developing cataloging rules in line with FRBR" was considered the most critical issue in the area of FRBR and related standards, but it also stands as the most critical issue in FRBR development, with the highest mean rating and strongest group consensus in the study. The development of such cataloging standards is seen as critical to implementing the FRBR model, especially within the library environment.

Additional issues in this area address specific standards critical to FRBR development, notably, standards for FRBR-based record structures, record encoding, and frameworks for FRBR implementation; FRBR-oriented authority work standards; standards to ensure interoperability for exchange and sharing of FRBR-based data; FRBR entity identifier standards; and display standards for FRBR implementations. The panel considered that such standards would enable or promote the use of FRBR by making the conceptual model implementable with specific guidelines.

SUMMARY

The FRBR report was published in 1998, but our current cataloging standards and practices have been slow to implement the changes. In order to implement the FRBR model, revisions of description standards are needed so that libraries might develop a better idea of how the model will change record structures and what information will be necessary to describe and provide access to the FRBR entities. Further, it would aid in developing interfaces and displays that will facilitate the FRBR-defined user tasks.

RDA is under development as an international standard for description and access, following the FRBR model, which places more emphasis on content versus the carrier (as AACR2 has done so far), covers both bibliographic and authority information, and encourages the application of FRBR and FRAD. MARC21 has been examined, and minor changes have been proposed. In addition, there is an exploration for the use of XML to encode bibliographic information.

It is still unclear how much change the new description standards will bring to cataloging practice. Speculation suggests that cataloging will be easier due to the elimination of duplicate description of works and expressions since each work and each expression will need to be described only once no matter how many manifestations are associated with them.

NOTES

1. International Standard Bibliographic Description (ISBD) / recommended by the ISBD Review Group; approved by the Standing Committee of the IFLA Cataloguing Section. — Preliminary consolidated ed. — München : K.G. Saur, 2007. — 1 vol. (loose-leaf) ; 32 cm. — (IFLA series on bibliographic control ; vol. 31). — ISBN 978-3-598-24280-9.

2. The conference proceedings have been published: The Principles and Future of AACR: Proceedings of the International Conference on the Principles and Future Development of AACR: Toronto, Ontario, Canada, October 23/25, 1997 / edited by Jean Weihs. — Ottawa: Canadian Library Association; London: Library Association Publishing; Chicago: American Library Association, 1998. — ISBN 0-88802-287-5 (ALA); 1-85604-303-7 (LA)

3. For related resources see Namespace for FRBR entities/elements in RDF: http://dublincore.org/dcmirdatask group/Namespace_20for_20FRBR_20entities_2felements_20in_20RDF

REFERENCES

Aalberg, Trond. 2007. "MARC and FRBR: Match or Mismatch?" Presentation at Cataloguing 2007: Back to Basics and Flying into the Future, Reykjavik Iceland, February 1–2, 2007. Available: www.congress.is/cataloguing2007 (accessed July 30, 2009).

American Library Association Committee on Cataloging: Description and Access. 2006. "RDA: Resource Description and Access. Part A, Chapters 6–7. Constituency Review of June 2006 Draft. ALA Response. September 25, 2006." Available: www.rda-jsc.org/docs/5rda-parta-ch6&7-alaresp.pdf (accessed July 30, 2009).

Bowen, Jennifer. 2005. "FRBR: Coming Soon to Your Library?" *Library Resources & Technical Services* 49, no. 3: 175–188.

The British Library. 2007. "Data Modeling, British Library, London, 30 April–1 May 2007." Available: www.bl.uk/bibliographic/meeting.html (accessed July 30, 2009).

Commissione Regole italiane di catalogazione per autori. 2009. Available: www.iccu.sbn.it/genera.jsp?id=94 (accessed July 30, 2009).

Coyle, Karen, and Diane Hillmann. 2007. "Resource Description and Access (RDA)." *D-Lib Magazine* 13, no. 1/2. Available: www.dlib.org/dlib/january07/coyle/01coyle.html (accessed July 30, 2009).

Davis, Ian, and Richard Newman. 2005. "Expression of Core FRBR Concepts in RDF." Available: http://vocab.org/frbr/core (accessed July 30, 2009).

Dublin Core Metadata Initiative/Resource Description and Access Task Group. 2008. "DCMI/RDA Task Group Wiki." Available: http://dublincore.org/dcmirdataskgroup/FrontPage (accessed July 30, 2009).

Hegna, Knut, and Eeva Murtomaa. 2003. "Data Mining MARC to Find: FRBR?" *International Cataloguing and Bibliographic Control: Quarterly Bulletin of the IFLA UBCIM Programme* 32, no. 3: 52–55.

International Conference on Cataloguing Principles (Paris: 1961). 1963. *Report.* London: International Federation of Library Associations and Institutions.

International Federation of Library Associations and Institutions Functional Requirements for Bibliographic Records Review Group. 2007. "Meeting Report, Held at the World Library and Information Congress in Durban, South Africa, 21 August 2007." Available: www.ifla.org/files/cataloguing/frbrrg/meeting_2007.pdf (accessed July 30, 2009).

International Federation of Library Associations and Institutions Functional Requirements for Bibliographic Records Review Group. 2008. "Declaring FRBR Entities and Relationships in RDF." Report on the FRBR Namespace Project, prepared by Gordon Dunsire. Available: www.ifla.org/files/cataloguing/frbrrg/namespace-report.pdf (accessed July 30, 2009).

International Federation of Library Associations and Institutions International Standard Bibliographic Description Review Group. 2004. *"Mapping ISBD Elements to FRBR Entity Attributes and Relationships."* Available: www.ifla.org/VII/s13/pubs/ISBD-FRBR-mappingFinal.pdf (accessed July 30, 2009).

International Federation of Library Associations and Institutions International Standard Bibliographic Description Review Group. 2008. [Homepage.] Available: www.ifla.org/en/isbd-rg (accessed July 30, 2009).

International Federation of Library Associations and Institutions Meeting of Experts on an International Cataloguing Code. 2008. "Statement of International Cataloguing Principles. Final Draft." Available: www.d-nb.de/standard isierung/afs/imeicc_papers.htm; www.d-nb.de/standardisierung/pdf/imeicc-statement_of_principles-2008.pdf (accessed July 30, 2009).

Library of Congress, National Library of Medicine, and National Agricultural Library. 2008. "Joint Statement of the Library of Congress, the National Library of Medicine, and the National Agricultural Library on Resource Description and Access." May 1, 2008. Available: www.loc.gov/bibliographic-future/news/RDA_Letter_050108.pdf (accessed July 30, 2009).

Joint Steering Committee for the Development of Resource Description and Access. 2009. "International Conference on the Principles & Future Development of AACR." Available: www.rda-jsc.org/intlconf1 .html (accessed July 30, 2009).

Joint Steering Committee for the Revision of *Anglo-American Cataloguing Rules*, Format Variation Working Group. 2002. "Discussion Paper 2002-DP08: Dealing with FRBR Expressions in MARC 21." Available: www.loc.gov/marc/marbi/2002/2002-dp08.html (accessed July 30, 2009).

McCallum, Sally H. 2005. "Using MARC 21 with FRBR: Record Configurations." Report to MARBI. Available: www.loc.gov/marc/marbi/2005/2005-report02.pdf (accessed July 30, 2009).

Network Development and MARC Standards Office (Library of Congress, NDMSO). 2006. "Functional Analysis of the MARC 21 Bibliographic and Holdings Formats: Library of Congress." Available: www.loc.gov/marc/marc-functional-analysis/functional-analysis .html (accessed July 30, 2009).

RDA/ONIX Initiative. 2008. [Homepage.] Available: www.rda-jsc.org/ rdaonixann.html (accessed July 30, 2009).

Regole italiane di catalogazione per autori Standing Commission. 2002. "The FRBR Model Application to Italian Cataloguing Practices: Problems and Use." *International Cataloguing and Bibliographic Control (ICBC)* 31, no. 2: 26–30.

Resource Description and Access/MARC Working Group. 2008. "Identifying Work and Expression Records in the MARC 21 Bibliographic and Authority Formats." *MARC Proposal No. 2008-05/2.* Available: www.loc .gov/marc/marbi/2008/2008-05-2.html (accessed July 30, 2009).

Styles, Rob, Danny Ayers, and Nadeem Shabir. 2008. "Semantic MARC, MARC21 and the Semantic Web." Paper presented at the WWW 2008 Workshop: Linked Data on the Web (LDOW2008), April 22, 2008, Beijing, China. Available: http://sunsite.informatik.rwth-aachen .de/ Publications/CEUR-WS/Vol-369/paper02.pdf (accessed July 30, 2009).

Svenonius, Elaine. 2000. *The Intellectual Foundation of Information Organization.* Cambridge, MA: MIT Press.

Tillett, Barbara B. 2005. "FRBR and Cataloging for the Future." *Cataloging & Classification Quarterly* 39, no. 3/4: 197–205.

Tillett, Barbara B. 2007a. "Cataloguing Codes and Conceptual Models: RDA and the Influence of FRBR and Other IFLA Initiatives." Presented at Cataloguing 2007: Back to Basics and Flying into the Future, Reykjavik Iceland, February 1–2, 2007. Available: www.congress.is/cataloguing2007 (accessed July 30, 2009).

Tillett, Barbara B. 2007b. "FRBR and RDA: Resource Description and Access." In *Understanding FRBR: What It Is and How It Will Affect Our Retrieval Tools* (pp. 87–95), edited by Arlene G. Taylor. Westport, CT: Libraries Unlimited.

Zhang, Yin, and Athena Salaba. 2009a. "FRBRizing Legacy Data: Issues and Challenges." 2009 ALA Midwinter Conference, ALA ALCTS CCS Cataloging Norms Interest Group, January 23–28, Denver, Colorado. Available: http://frbr.slis.kent.edu/presentations.htm (accessed July 30, 2009).

Zhang, Yin, and Athena Salaba. 2009b. "What Is Next for FRBR? A Delphi Study." *The Library Quarterly* 79, no. 2: 233–255.

►4

FRBR APPLICATION

The FRBR (Functional Requirements for Bibliographic Records) model can be applied to a variety of settings and collections, including both format-based collections and domain-specific collections. A number of benefits have been identified for both the end user of a library catalog and the library staff. Such benefits include easier searching, focused results, clustering at the work level, understanding and using bibliographic relationships, and better navigation of the catalog for end users (Noerr et al, 1998). Additional benefits for library staff include better placement of data in records, more efficient copy cataloging and sharing of records, and the faster addition of new data such as rights management (Noerr et al, 1998).

Though many benefits of the FRBR model have been identified, the application of the FRBR model is expected to be more beneficial to certain types of resources. In general, collections thought to benefit the most are those consisting of works expressed in a variety of ways or published in different editions, by different publishers, in different mediums, etc. These include collections of fictional works, music collections, serial collections, and other aggregate works. In other words, the model will be most advantageous for users who are looking for works with many expressions and manifestations, but not as advantageous for those looking for works with one expression and very few manifestations.

Following is a brief overview of FRBR applications as related to various types of collections and differing information environments with a brief description and discussion of some of the issues that have been identified for each area.

COLLECTIONS: GENRE/FORMAT AND DISCIPLINARY COMMUNITIES

The FRBR model has been applied to collections of literature, classical texts, fiction, serials and other continuing resources, works of art, music, moving images, and the performing arts. The information that follows is based either on current literature, discussion related to these types of collections, or from FRBRization projects themselves.

Works of Art, Cultural Objects

Works of art are unique cultural objects, and often the definition of work in this environment does not necessarily coincide with the definition of work in FRBR. Cultural objects such as buildings and other art works are physical objects or are associated with a physical instantiation, present or past, whereas the FRBR work exists only as an abstract idea. In addition, based on the *Cataloging Cultural Objects* (CCO), the cataloging standard for works of art, most objects do not fit the work, expression, and manifestation model (Baca and Clarke, 2007). For example, under CCO, different versions of a painting, including early drawings, are considered separate works, while under FRBR they would be considered different expressions. Similarly, prints of a painting are considered by CCO to be different but related works rather than manifestations. There is one strong commonality between CCO and FRBR: the importance of relationships. According to Baca and Clarke (2007), the FRBR model might be more useful for reproductions of works of art.

Traditionally, works of art are described using an object-oriented model. These works are single-object entities that are related to many other objects. In an examination of the feasibility of applying the FRBR model to describe objects of art at the National Palace Museum in Taipei, Chen and Chen (2004) concluded that the FRBR primary relationships (between Group 1 entities) could be used to express the relationships between works and their reproductions. On the other hand, horizontal relationships to show how two works are related are also necessary in this environment.

Therefore, they suggested that an expansion of FRBR relationships might be necessary if the model is to be applied to the description of and access to works of art.

Classical Texts

Latin and classical Greek texts have also been the subject of FRBRization discussions. Like art, collections of classical texts include many works related to other works. In addition, classical works illustrate the case in which numerous differing expressions and manifestations exist for the same work. The Perseus Digital Library (PDL) has done an extensive study on how to apply the FRBR model to classical texts to create a hierarchical catalog (Mimno, Crane, and Jones, 2005). PDL's application of FRBR to its classical texts collection reveals that the collection is a good candidate for FRBR implementation as the collection would benefit from a hierarchical catalog, where manifestations are linked to expressions and works and vice versa. Another benefit of applying FRBR to these types of materials is the emphasis not only on work-to-work relationships but also, to a large degree, on linkages through part-whole and whole-part relationships. One of the issues that might prove challenging is that often a particular manifestatio`n needs to be linked to a large number of expressions/works due to a large number of anthologies and selections that include multiple works. Therefore, a good taxonomy of relationships and a solid structure for linking manifestations to multiwork and multiexpression records are necessary for successful application of the FRBR model to collections of classical texts.

Fiction

Fictional works are thought to be the materials that will benefit most from the application of the FRBR model. These collections include works with a number of expressions, often with several manifestations under each expression, and relationships to other works such as adaptations. Collections of fiction have been the subject of experimentations for FRBRization projects such as the work on *Humphry Clinker* by O'Neill (2002) and Abbott's *Flatland* by Ercegovac (2006). The application of FRBR to *Humphry Clinker* proved to be a complicated process due to the fact that existing catalog records do not include sufficient information for distinguishing expression or for linking manifestations to the correct expression. The study concludes that "[t]he irony is that the FRBR model provides minimal benefits to the small works that can be reliably FRBRized, but fails on the large and complex works where it is most needed" (O'Neill, 2002: 159). Similarly, Ercegovac (2006) found that information in current catalog records lack details about the type of expression and linkages to both the original publication and the work. Both of these studies examined the application of FRBR using existing catalog records that had not been created based on the FRBR model.

It is hoped that the application of FRBR, through a FRBR-based standard of description, will benefit these large and complex fictional works. FRBR application has the potential to differentiate among the various expressions of these works and to allow for easier navigation through all of their expressions and manifestations as well as through other related works. In order to achieve this, special attention must be given to relationships, responsibilities and the roles of responsible parties, and the use of uniform titles. One of the strengths of FRBR is the added emphasis on relationships. What might be problematic are the development of standards that will mandate responsibility roles and the use of uniform titles for linking works, expressions, and manifestations. In current cataloging practices, uniform titles have two functions: (1) as a work title, which allows linking expressions under the work; and (2) as a collocative title, which may link a number of works (such as *Works*), selections of a work, or works of the same genre/format (such as *Poems*, *Essays*, etc.). These two different functions need to be separated in order to be able to correctly link manifestations to appropriate expressions and works. *Resource Description and Access* (RDA), the description standard based on FRBR that is currently under development, has been criticized for not making this distinction and continuing the current practice, which might hinder the proper application of the FRBR model to fictional works.

One of the earliest and largest FRBR applications to fictional works is OCLC's (Online Computer Library Center) creation of FictionFinder, a research prototype based on WorldCat's collection that provides access to books, e-books, and audiobooks that have been coded as fiction (see also description in Chapter 5). Fiction has been defined as fictional prose to include novels and short stories but with very minimal inclusion of fiction in poetry, drama, comics, and graphic novels (Beall and Vizine-Goetz, 2006). This prototype uses OCLC's Work-Set Algorithm and, therefore, the collection is retrieved in work-view clusters. Some elements are used to further group the work-based results into editions (a mix of expression and manifestation-based groupings). This might reflect the identified and discussed challenges with distinguishing expressions from manifestations and linking a manifestation to a particular expression and might offer one application and system implementation solution to this issue.

Hand-Press Materials

Applying the FRBR model to hand-press materials might prove problematic and even nonbeneficial. One major issue is the specificity of the definition of the expression entity (Jonsson, 2005). Variations during the production process of hand-press materials can result in a number of slightly differing versions among copies of the same edition, and according to the original FRBR report these would constitute different expressions. In addition, in FRBR, all copies of a manifestation are identical, which is not true in the case of hand-press items due to the differences in the settings for the reproduction process. Considering all of the problems with expression and manifestation definitions in FRBR and the differences in hand-press materials, Jonsson suggests that a combination of the work and item FRBR entities along with the current terms of edition, issue, and state would better serve description of these materials and users' needs in finding materials and browsing these collections. In conclusion, Jonsson proposes leaving the definition of expression to a more general level of identification rather than to a specific one (Jonsson, 2005).

Literature (National)

National literature with an author-centered focus has also been the subject of FRBR application. This is different from fiction collections in that it includes not only literary works and traditionally published works but also information about the authors and their works from a variety of sources. These sources may include whole monographs, separate works inside a monograph's carrier, anthologies, newspapers, journals, Web sites, individual non-monograph items, series, and other sequences. The focus of these collections is the writings of a country, similar to a national bibliography. The best example in this area is AustLit's[1] effort to provide access to all works by and literary criticism of Australian authors as well the compilation of all pertinent information about the career, work, and life of each author. In this case, one of the FRBR Group 1 entities is not included in the catalog—the item entity. Item level information is stored in the traditional library holdings of each individual library when needed. During AustLit's application of FRBR to their national literature collection, a number of modifications or additional considerations and solutions to the model were necessary. For example, Ayres, Fitch, and Kilner (2003) state that since FRBR was developed mainly with monographs in mind, this particular application had to expand the model to fit the needs of many other types of works. These expansions include the ideas borrowed from ABC Harmony and INDECS that works have a creation event, expressions have a realization event, and manifestations have an embodiment event.

Live Performing Arts

Live performances are sets of works. Recorded live performances are dealt with in current description standards, but live performances are not. Currently, libraries accommodate these descriptions in different ways due to the lack of standardization. It is hoped that the theory behind the FRBR model will drive the standardization of the description of live performances. Miller and Le Boeuf (2005) examined two applications of FRBR to live performances, one at the Dance Heritage Coalition and the other at the National Library of France. They concluded that the FRBR model can be used for the description of performing arts but that a number of expansions will be necessary. Again, the expression entity is different for this type of resource in that each dance performance is an expression of the choreographer's choreographic work and the actors perform an expression of the director's spatio-temporal work, which is itself based on the playwright's textual work. In addition, the model needs to account for the chronological structure of live performance creations, which includes runs, revivals, and the sum of all runs and revivals. The authors suggest that one could map all of these to the Group 1 entities, but then the question is raised of whether or not forcing the model to accommodate the description of a particular type of resource will best serve the needs of all users.

Finally, live performances are a unique type of collection in that libraries do not hold copies of the same performance of a work and must instead link to materials related through other types of bibliographic relationships. Related materials may include photographs, programs, costumes, clippings, manuscripts, and choreographic notations (Miller and Le Boeuf, 2005).

Moving Images

There are several issues involving moving image cataloging and how moving images fit into the FRBR model. Yee (1993) called for attention in four different types of alterations, which may be considered changes in expressions or manifestations. These alterations include changes in footage, changes in continuity, changes in the textual aspect of the film, and changes in performance. Since FRBR as a model does not include guidelines to distinguish such differences nor to identify them as new expressions or new manifestations, this is an important issue that will require cataloging standards to address it.

Another important issue is the distinction between content (mapping to FRBR work and expression entities) and container or carrier (mapping to the FRBR manifestation). Yee (2007) states that the FRBR definition of work is in line with the one used by film catalogers. Moving image works are visual works and not textual or musical works; therefore, any changes that happen to the textual or musical parts and are then transformed into a visual work constitute a new work. Any change that happens in the content of the visual work would constitute a new expression. Cataloging standards will need to pay special attention to the work and expression relationships for moving images, as the model lacks clarity in the expression and manifestation entities when it comes to moving images. There is a need to clarify which physical elements are to be considered content elements and which are carrier elements. Changes in content create a new expression; changes in carrier create a new manifestation. The inability to distinguish between intentional and unintentional content changes represents another gap in the FRBR model. "Unintentional/malicious content changes should not be held to create new expressions," rather, they are a special kind of manifestation (Yee, 2007: 120).

Also, it is necessary to distinguish between film and video expressions and film- and video-related adaptations within this category of materials. One issue arises in accessing the same film stored in different containers, for which current cataloging rules require the creation and display of individual bibliographic records. At the UCLA Film and Television Archive (see description in Chapter 5), this issue has been resolved by including manifestation information in the holdings record instead of in the bibliographic record (Yee, 2005).

Music

Music collections are another area that can greatly benefit from the application of FRBR. Due to the nature of these materials, it is not easy to define the boundaries of relevant works and expressions. Music can be represented as notation-based, text-based, audio-based, or audiovisual-based (Vellucci, 2007). Different types of musical works include individual works, aggregated musical works, fragments of musical works, and works of vocal music (Le Boeuf, 2005).

There are a few issues with the FRBR definition of work as it relates to music. Music has both simple and complex works. Often these are aggregate works or unified works. Aggregate works are works that are composed of independent components, while unified works have two types of semantic content that are integrated to exist as one work (Vellucci, 2007). Le Boeuf (2005) states that because the work is abstract, it is difficult to set boundaries and therefore to distinguish between work and expression when dealing with musical works. The other issue is determining the primacy of a work when it contains more than one type of semantic contents (Vellucci, 2007). In the example of a poem that is set to music, are the lyrics the primary work or is the music the primary work?

Current cataloging practices might also become an issue when trying to apply the FRBR model to musical works. Uniform titles often are used not only to identify works but also as a genre-based collocating device, such as "Symphonies" and "Violin music." These often have additional elements that combine work and expression information. Relator codes are often missing from our current records and will be of great importance in the application of FRBR to music. In addition, an extensive list of bibliographic relationships exists among entities within music collections that are not necessarily part of FRBR.

Oral Tradition Works

The oral tradition work (OTW) can be transmitted through one of three methods. In the first method, the oral tradition transmits the one and only version of a myth, as it has always existed. In the second method of oral tradition, version follows version but they are not identical, even though everyone pretends that they are. In this case, the myth is not considered a finite resource but a continuously integrating resource. In the third oral tradition method, version follows version where these versions are highly similar and coexist in people's minds or in information systems. In this last tradition the notion of a work is very necessary because there are many versions that are explicitly to be collocated (Nicolas, 2005).

Nicolas (2005) states that the application of FRBR allows a better treatment of works within oral traditions. One issue involved with these collections is FRBR's definition of work and the compatibility of expressions with the different versions of these works. FRBR's definition of a work as being the content common among variations is not a good one for oral tradition works, as demonstrated by anthropologists. Therefore, changes in the definition of "work" are necessary. In addition, it is essential that more attention be given to "versions" and their relationships. Versions do not always derive from one original source but from a series of versions. The relationship between versions is not covered in FRBR.

Serials, Other Continuing Resources, and Aggregates

Serials and other types of continuing resources (hereafter referred to collectively as serials) have been the subject of much discussion with regard to the application of FRBR. Among the discussions for applying FRBR to serials are the issues of seriality, serials as aggregated works, format variation (multiple versions of the same journal), and the issue of frequent journal title changes (Antelman, 2004).

Even though many believe that serials fit the Group 1 entity work, it is the consensus that serials are a work of collected or aggregated works. The FRBR Final Report does not explicitly cover serials, especially in the examples used to illustrate the different entities and attributes. This lack of coverage has led to differing interpretations of the model when it comes to whether a journal article is a work in itself or an independent part of a whole work. The relationships between work, part of a work, expression, manifestation, and item are complex in the serials environment (Johnson, 2006). As a result, Shadle (2007) stated that the FRBR entities and relationships could not be easily adapted to serials. Seriality is also not covered in FRBR in a way that would be helpful to serial catalogers but rather only through some of the defined attributes such as extensibility and intended termination.

In current cataloging practice a name/title key through the main entry and the uniform title usually identifies monographic works. These two elements are, according to Antelman (2004), weak identifiers for serials. For serials, the title is currently the element used for identification of the work; thus, based on cataloging practices, every time there is a change in the title of a serial it is treated as a new work. This is very confusing to the cataloger and even more so to end users, who do not think the same way about changes in serial titles. An additional problem with current practice is that in the chain of a serial's title changes, linkages are made only between titles that immediately precede or follow a given title and not between all of a serial's titles. Serials also might not fit into the FRBR model because they have a much greater range of Group 1 entity relationships than those defined by FRBR, such as "successor" and "supplement" relationships, and therefore a more comprehensive theory of serial aggregates is needed. The issues involved with aggregate works are currently under further development by the FRBR Working Group on Aggregates.

Overall, it seems that the definition of work, the lack of clear treatment of serials as works or aggregate works in FRBR, the issues of seriality and serials identifiers (title, uniform title, etc.), and the need for additional attributes and relationships indicate that more needs to be done to expand the FRBR model for successful application of the model to serials.

SETTINGS

FRBR was developed by the library community to better serve user tasks. However, this does not mean that FRBR is applicable only within traditional libraries. Other and more specialized settings for the potential application of FRBR have been discussed among the international community. The following sections describe some examples of such settings.

Traditional Libraries

FRBR was developed within the library community to help identify the functional requirements for library bibliographic records. Therefore, the main audience of the FRBR report, and the most likely setting in which to apply the model, is the traditional library environment. Cataloging standards, such as RDA, are under development and existing standards are being modified to incorporate the FRBR model. Also, a number of experimental library projects are underway to examine the feasibility of and develop processes for the application and implementation of FRBR. Such examples include the E-Matrix project (www.lib.ncsu.edu/ e-matrix) at the North Carolina State University Libraries (NCSU) to implement the model, particularly for electronic resource management, the University of Rochester libraries with the application of FRBR to its music and video collections, and the development of a new FRBR-based catalog, the eXtensible Catalog (XC) (www.extensiblecatalog.org).

Consortia

Libraries often participate in networks or consortia for record and resource sharing. One issue that arises is whether FRBR will make record sharing easier or more difficult. Examples of issues to be resolved include deciding what information should be part of the bibliographic record and what information should be in the authority record. At what level should we create records: work level, expression level, manifestation level, or all of these? It is hoped that some of these issues will be resolved with the development of guidelines and cataloging standards. Examples of consortia that have been experimenting with the application of the FRBR model to their union catalogs include OCLC's WorldCat (http://worldcat.org), which has implemented some FRBR concepts to the WorldCat collection; the LibraryLabs project of Libraries Australia (http://ll01.nla.gov.au), a prototype using a copy of the Australian National Bibliographic Database (ANBD) to group MARC records into a FRBR-like structure; and AustLit (www.austlit.edu.au), a collaboration between 12 Australian universities and the National Library of Australia that implemented FRBR to describe and provide access to literary and creative works.

Digital Libraries

Those conducting a number of digital library projects are interested in applying the FRBR model to their data to create hierarchical catalogs, but so far there is limited discussion of digital library implementation of FRBR. Dunn and others discuss using the FRBR model for metadata in a music digital library (Dunn et al., 2006). Weng and Mi discuss using FRBR for a digital library of images of cultural objects (Weng and Mi, 2006). One distinguishing characteristic of many digital libraries is that they are not using the same standards for description or encoding that traditional libraries use, e.g., MARC and AACR2. Digital libraries provide access to a variety of dynamic materials and typically need to have more detailed descriptions and additional types of information regarding preservation, rights management, structural information, and use information. Many digital libraries see the application of FRBR as an opportunity to increase interoperability between traditional settings, such as libraries, and diverse settings, such as digital libraries. Examples of digital libraries that are exploring the application of FRBR include the Perseus Digital Library (www.perseus.tufts.edu/hopper) of classical texts and the Variations projects for the digital music library collections at Indiana University.

Institutional Repositories

Many universities and other institutions are charged with the management, preservation, dissemination, and provision of access to institutional and scholarly assets via a single repository. Several challenges are involved with institutional repositories due to the variety of assets and the different functional requirements for each type of asset to be included. These repositories could greatly improve their accessibility and quality with the application of FRBR. Kim and Kim examined using the FRBR model to cluster and display related materials in dCollection, a consortium of Korean university institutional repositories, and suggest that such clustering improves its usability (Kim and Kim, 2008).

Internet Archives

One major challenge with the Internet is the fluidity of Web resource content and the multiple versions of each resource. There is great potential to solve many of these issues by exploring how to best apply the FRBR model to this setting. Norway's Paradigma Project is the first project to explore the application of FRBR to a digital culture archive. In the process of applying the FRBR model to Paradigma's collection of archived Web documents, it was deemed necessary to make modifications to the *manifestation* and *item* entities in order to adequately describe the temporal information related to this type of resources. Unfortunately, no current information about Paradigma is available.

Museums

This environment differs from the traditional library setting because it collects unique works of art and often uses an object-oriented model for the representation of resources. Due to the similar aspects of libraries and museums, there is a great effort toward harmonizing the entity-relationship FRBR model with the object-oriented CRM model of the International Council of Museums (http://cidoc.ics.forth.gr). The National Palace Museum in Taipei (www.npm.gov.tw/en/home.htm) examined the application of FRBR in describing Chinese paintings and calligraphy and to differentiate originals artworks and reproductions. It was concluded that FRBR's *work* and *expression* entities are in line with the museum's emphasis on work and expression and use of the Categories for the Description of Works of Art (CDWA) to create metadata for this particular collection.

CRITICAL ISSUES AND CHALLENGES IN FRBR APPLICATION

As noted in Chapter 1, the FRBR Delphi panel identified a number of issues regarding the application of the FRBR model to different collections and settings. Foremost among these issues is the lack of guidelines and examples for application. As a conceptual model, FRBR does not offer any guidelines for particular applications or rules for describing resources in a variety of domains and settings. Related to this issue is the fact that professionals interested in applying the model do not always have a clear understanding of it or may interpret the model's intention incorrectly, which may result in inappropriate applications. The panel recognized that the application of the model may vary to fit the needs of particular settings and therefore called for community based application profiles (Zhang and Salaba, 2009).

SUMMARY

The FRBR model was developed within the library community, but with the intention that it could be applied to a variety of information communities. A number of discussions and projects are taking place, focusing on the applicability of the FRBR model to specific collections, settings, and domains. It is speculated that collections of monographic works with numerous expressions and manifestations, musical collections, and fictional collections may benefit the most from the application of the FRBR model. Other collections that may benefit from the FRBR application include moving images, classical texts, works of art, and serial publications. Each of these collections has specific needs for additional information in their descriptions, and development of additional relationships between entities, mainly in the form of expanded definitions of the entity work and expression, is necessary. The FRBR model, even though published in 1998, is continually reviewed by different communities and through review groups that work on specific issues related to the expansion of the model to better fit other collections and to increase its applicability to different information settings. These settings include museums, digital libraries, Internet archives, and consortia.

NOTE

1. www.austlit.edu.au: "AustLit provides authoritative information on Australian creative and critical literature works as well as authors and literary organizations."

REFERENCES

Antelman, Kristin. 2004. "Identifying the Serial Work As a Bibliographic Entity." *Library Resources & Technical Services* 48, no. 4: 238–255.

Ayres, Marie-Louise, Kent Fitch, and Kerry Kilner. 2003. "Report on the Successful AustLit: Australian Literature Gateway Implementation of the FRBR and INDECS Event Models, and Implications for Other FRBR Implementations." *International Cataloguing and Bibliographic Control: Quarterly Bulletin of the IFLA UBCIM Programme* 32, no. 1: 8–13.

Baca, Murtha, and Sherman Clarke. 2007. "FRBR and Works of Art, Architecture, and Material Culture." In *Understanding FRBR: What It Is and How It Will Affect Our Retrieval Tools* (pp. 103–110), edited by Arlene G. Taylor. Westport, CT: Libraries Unlimited.

Beall, Juanne, and Diane Vizine-Goetz. 2006. "Finding Fiction: Facilitating Access to Works of the Imagination Scattered by Form and Format." Paper presented at the Ninth International ISKO Conference, 7 July 2006, Vienna (Austria). Available: www.oclc.org/research/staff/vizine-goetz.htm (accessed July 30, 2009).

Chen, Yaning, and Shu-jiun Chen. 2004. "A Metadata Practice of the IFLA FRBR Model: A Case Study for the National Palace Museum in Taipei." *Journal of Documentation* 60, no. 2: 128–143.

Dunn, Jon W., Donald Byrd, Mark Notess, Jenn Riley, and Ryan Scherle. 2006. "Variations2: Retrieving and Using Music in an Academic Setting." *Communications of the ACM* (August): 53–58.

Ercegovac, Zorana. 2006. "Multiple-Version Resources in Digital Libraries: Towards User-Centered Displays." *Journal of the American Society for Information Science and Technology* 57, no. 8: 1023–1032.

International Federation of Library Associations and Institutions Study Group on the Functional Requirements for Bibliographic Records. 1998. *Functional Requirements for Bibliographic Records: Final Report.* Munich, Germany: K. G. Saur. Available: www.ifla.org/en/publications/functional-requirements-for-bibliographic-records (accessed July 30, 2009).

Johnson, Kay G. 2006. "Serials: The Constant Midlife Crisis." *Serials Review* 32, no. 1: 35–39.

Jonsson, Gunilla. 2005. "Cataloguing of Hand Press Materials and the Concept of Expression in FRBR." *Cataloging & Classification Quarterly* 39, no. 3/4: 77–86.

Kim, Hyun Hee, and Yong Ho Kim. 2008. "Usability Study of Digital Institutional Repositories." *The Electronic Library* 26, no. 6: 863–881.

Le Boeuf, Patrick. 2005. "Musical Works in the FRBR Model or 'Quasi la Stessa Cosa': Variations on a Theme by Umberto Eco." *Cataloging & Classification Quarterly* 39, no. 3/4: 103–124.

Miller, David, and Patrick Le Boeuf. 2005. "'Such Stuff as Dreams Are Made On': How Does FRBR Fit Performing Arts?" *Cataloging & Classification Quarterly* 39, no. 3/4: 151–78.

Mimno, David, Gregory Crane, and Alison Jones. 2005. "Hierarchical Catalog Records: Implementing a FRBR Catalog." *D-Lib Magazine* 11, no. 10: 1. Available: www.dlib.org/dlib/october05/crane/10crane.html (accessed July 30, 2009).

Nicolas, Yann. 2005. "Folklore Requirements for Bibliographic Records: Oral Traditions and FRBR." *Cataloging & Classification Quarterly* 39, no. 3/4: 179–195.

Noerr, Peter, Paula Goossens, Dan Matei, Petra Otten, Susanna Peruginelli, and Maria Witt. 1998. "User Benefits from a New Bibliographic Model: Follow-Up of the IFLA Functional Requirements Study." *International Cataloguing and Bibliographic Control: Quarterly Bulletin of the IFLA UBCIM Programme* 28, no. 3: 80–81. Available: http://archive .ifla.org/IV/ifla64/084-126e.htm (accessed July 30, 2009).

O'Neill, Edward T. 2002. "FRBR: Functional Requirements for Bibliographic Records: Application of the Entity-Relationship Model to Humphry Clinker." *Library Resources & Technical Services* 46, no. 4:150–159.

Shadle, Steven C. 2007. "FRBR and Serials: One Serialist's Analysis." In *Understanding FRBR: What It Is and How It Will Affect Our Retrieval Tools* (pp. 153–174), edited by Arlene G. Taylor. Westport, CT: Libraries Unlimited.

Vellucci, Sherry L. 2007. "FRBR and Music." In *Understanding FRBR: What It Is and How It Will Affect Our Retrieval Tools* (pp. 131–151), edited by Arlene G. Taylor. Westport, CT: Libraries Unlimited.

Weng, Cathy, and Jia Mi. 2006. "Towards Accessibility to Digital Cultural Materials: A FRBRized Approach." *OCLC Systems & Services* 22, no. 3: 217–232.

Yee, Martha M. 1993. "The Concept of Work for Moving Image Materials." *Cataloging & Classification Quarterly* 18, no. 2: 33–40.

Yee, Martha M. 2005. "FRBRization: A Method for Turning Online Public Finding Lists into Online Public Catalogs." *Information Technology and Libraries* 24, no. 3: 77–95.

Yee, Martha M. 2007. "FRBR and Moving Image Materials: Content (Work and Expression) versus Carrier (Manifestation)." In *Understanding FRBR: What Is It and How It Will Affect Our Retrieval Tools* (pp. 117–129), edited by Arlene G. Taylor. Westport, CT: Libraries Unlimited.

Zhang, Yin, and Athena Salaba. 2009. "What Is Next for FRBR? A Delphi Study." *The Library Quarterly* 79, no. 2: 233–255.

▶5

FRBR IMPLEMENTATIONS IN LIBRARY CATALOGS

F RBR (Functional Requirements for Bibliographic Records) provides great opportunities for creating retrieval systems that better support user information seeking. Various efforts are underway to explore methods for implementing this model in a way that creates more effective retrieval systems. Because FRBR is essentially a conceptual model, and there have not been specific guidelines or even best practices established for FRBR implementations, current efforts are largely exploratory in nature. These efforts vary in scope, ranging from

- ▶ having theoretical discussions to conducting practical evaluations and making recommendations of possible implementation approaches,
- ▶ creating prototype systems for research and evaluation purposes to creating fully functional systems in service, and
- ▶ developing algorithms and support software as part of the FRBR implementation process to developing a full suite of software for building a FRBR system.

Overall, current FRBR implementations can be divided into two broad categories: (1) implementing FRBR in online library catalogs (either general library collections or specific types of library collections) and (2) implementing FRBR in nontraditional library settings, such as special collections, museums, digital collections, archives, and Internet resources as discussed in Chapter 4.

Due to the scope and targeted audiences of this book, this chapter will focus on FRBR implementations related to library catalogs. It will provide an overview of current FRBR implementation efforts through a survey and examination of FRBR development projects for catalogs. These FRBR projects showcase the implementation of FRBR for different purposes through variations in FRBR model focus, system collection, record creation and FRBRization, system user interface and display, system architecture and other technical details, and user evaluation and testing. This chapter also discusses specific issues that have been or need to be addressed for future implementation and development.

CURRENT FRBR IMPLEMENTATION PROJECTS

The FRBR implementation projects related to library catalogs that the authors of this book surveyed and evaluated involve the actual creation and development of working FRBR-based full-scale systems, prototypes or experimental systems, or algorithms and software for FRBR implementations. These various types of projects are described below:

> ► *Full-scale systems.* Some FRBR-based systems are full-scale working systems, such as WorldCat.org, developed by Online Computer Library Center (OCLC) and the University of California at Los Angeles (UCLA) Film and Television Archive OPAC (Online Public Access Catalog), which are production systems that support regular services and functions.

> ► *Prototypes or experimental systems.* Some FRBR-based systems are prototypes or experimental test systems developed to explore FRBR implementations. These systems do not support real live library services. For example, LibraryLabs of Libraries Australia (http://ll01.nla.gov.au), a FRBR prototype developed by National Library of Australia, illustrates prototype service with stale data rather than its production service.

> ► *Algorithms and software.* Along with implementing FRBR catalog systems, some projects develop algorithms and software to facilitate FRBR implementations. Such algorithms and software may help create an entire system or focus on certain aspects of the system, such as FRBRization of MARC records or the

creation of user interfaces based on the FRBR model. For example, OCLC has developed the FRBR Work-Set Algorithm, which FRBRizes MARC records at the work entity level. The Library of Congress has developed the FRBR Display Tool, which allows libraries to display their resources by clustering bibliographic records according to the FRBR model.

It should be noted that current FRBR systems for library catalogs are essentially FRBRized systems based on existing MARC records or systems that conform to FRBR rather than newly created FRBR systems independent of current records and systems. Also, the FRBR algorithms and software are largely developed to FRBRize existing data and systems. Below is a brief summary of individual FRBR implementation projects based on three categories: (1) full-scale systems, (2) prototypes or experimental systems, and (3) algorithms and software for FRBR implementation.

Full-Scale Systems

WorldCat.org

Developer: OCLC
URL(s): www.worldcat.org
The WorldCat database is the largest and most comprehensive union catalog in the world. As of March 2009, WorldCat.org contains over 1.2 billion items, including following types of materials: (1) traditional library materials, such as popular books, music CDs, and videos; (2) new kinds of digital content such as downloadable digital audiobooks; (3) article citations with links to their full text; (4) authoritative research materials such as documents and photos of local or historic significance; and (5) digital versions of rare items that are not available to the public (OCLC WorldCat, 2009, www .worldcat.org/whatis/default.jsp). Because WorldCat is essentially a worldwide union catalog, resources are available in many languages.

WorldCat.org utilizes the OCLC Work-Set Algorithm to FRBRize the collection by grouping records by *work*. The project uses FRBR concepts such as *work*, *expression*, and *manifestation* to explore how records should cluster in order to ease and quicken a user's search for relevant materials. For example, it reduces the number of

▶ FIGURE 5-1. An Example of a WorldCat.org Search Result Display

Source: Screenshot of OCLC WorldCat.org search results is ©2009 OCLC Online Computer Library Center. Inc. WorldCat, the WorldCat logo, and WorldCat.org are trademarks and/or service marks of OCLC.

editions on the results screen. WorldCat also offers some common Web search features such as a faceted display for refining a search result set. The screen in Figure 5-1 shows the result of a search for Arlene Taylor's *The Organization of Information*, which is a work. The first hit is relevant, although it is not a FRBR work in the real sense since it has a specific format, publisher, and year attached to it. But compared to regular online catalogs, this display is helpful in that it offers users links to collocate and view all editions and formats along with facet-based refinement options by specific author, format, year, and language on the left side of the screen.

UCLA Film and Television Archive OPAC

Developer: UCLA Film and Television Archive

URL(s): http://cinema.library.ucla.edu

The UCLA Film and Television Archive is the second largest media materials collection in the United States. According to the project launch announcement made by project leader Martha Yee (2007), the new online catalog interface incorporates the FRBR model using the traditional integrated library system—Endeavor Information Systems' Voyager ILS. In this FRBR-based catalog, an authority record is treated as a work record, a bibliographic record as an expression record, and a holdings record as a manifestation record for various format and distribution information. The screen in Figure 5-2 shows the results of a title search for the work *Gone with the Wind*. Several works are retrieved, including the work with "Gone with the wind (Motion picture)" in the uniform title field. In this case, three expressions of the work (the original film, the fiftieth anniversary edition, and the collector's edition) are displayed together (records [2-4]). The third expression record (record [4]) is illustrated in Figure 5-3, which shows its two manifestations. This catalog offers displays that allow search results to be consolidated, with multiple expressions grouped together in the initial search display of works and multiple manifestations of an expression listed together in that expression's record, which helps simplify the users' collocating process. To

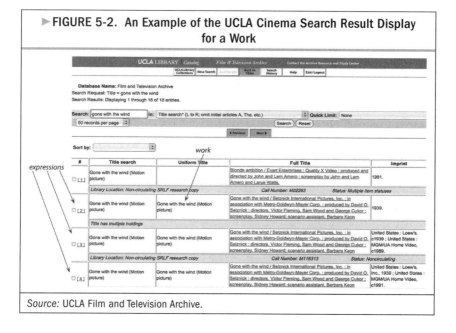

▷ **FIGURE 5-2. An Example of the UCLA Cinema Search Result Display for a Work**

Source: UCLA Film and Television Archive.

▶ **FIGURE 5-3. An Example of UCLA Cinema Expression and Manifestation Records**

	Confederate States of America --History --Drama.
Genre(s)/Form(s):	Academy Award films.
	Historical re-creations.
	Features.
Credits heading(s):	Selznick, David O., 1902-1965. production
	Fleming, Victor, 1883-1949. direction
	Leigh, Vivien, 1913-1967. cast
	Gable, Clark, 1901-1960. cast
	Mitchell, Margaret, 1900-1949. Gone with the wind.
	Gone with the wind (Motion picture)--trailer. Pre-release trailer.
BBID (expression):	44594
Database:	Film and Television Archive

expression

Location:	NON-CIRCULATING RESEARCH AND STUDY CENTER COPY
Inventory Number:	VD358 M
Collection:	MP Motion Picture Collection
Format:	5 videodiscs of 5 (laser optical CAV) (222 min.) : sd., col. ; 12 in.
Notes:	NOTES: "c1939, Turner Entertainment Co.; Package design c1991 MGM/UA Home Video, Inc. and Turner Entertainment Co."
	Rev. March 25, 2003, my.
HLDID (manifestation):	74459

manifestations

Location:	NON-CIRCULATING RESEARCH AND STUDY CENTER COPY
Inventory Number:	VD763 M
Collection:	MP Motion Picture Collection
Format:	5 videodiscs of 5 (laser optical CAV) (222 min.) : sd., col. ; 12 in.
Notes:	Study copy. Available for onsite viewing only.
	Input March 25, 2003, my.
HLDID (manifestation):	270788

Source: UCLA Film and Television Archive.

---

some extent, it supports hierarchical browsing and display of works, expressions, and manifestations, although it requires multiple clicks for users to actually go through the hierarchy and some interpretation of the expression and manifestation information in the expression record is necessary.

Prototypes or Experimental Systems

OCLC FictionFinder

Developer: OCLC

URL(s): http://fictionfinder.oclc.org

FictionFinder is a FRBR research prototype that provides access to 2.8 million works of fiction in the form of books, e-books, and audio materials in the WorldCat database (OCLC, 2007, http://fictionfinder.oclc.org). FictionFinder uses the OCLC FRBR Work-Set Algorithm to group together records that represent the same work in a set called a work-set. It supports searches not only through common catalog search options such as title, author, and subject, but also by some fiction-specific information such as fictitious characters, literary awards, and book summaries. Search results are organized by work and ranked by holdings. Figure 5-4 illustrates the results of a title keyword search for "Hamlet" that yields 139 works. The first hit is the work Hamlet by Shakespeare with 349 editions—a user-friendly term used in FictionFinder for manifestations. When this work is selected for further information, the user is presented with a display showing a mixture of expressions and manifestations that are derived from this particular work (see Figure 5-5, previous page). This FRBR view helps users to browse search results and to understand how retrieved records are related to one another. In addition, this interface allows users to refine the resulting display by language and format and to sort by any attribute in the tabular headings to dynamically reorganize search results, which may help users evaluate, locate, and select what they are seeking.

▶ **FIGURE 5-4. The OCLC FictionFinder Search Result Display by Work**

You searched: Title for **hamlet**

Previous 10 Works   Displaying 1 - 10 of 139   Next 10 Works >>   Jump to work: 1

Title / Author	Editions	Libraries ▾
1. **Hamlet** / Shakespeare, William Distressed by his father's death and his mother's over-hasty remarriage, Hamlet, Prince of Denmark is faced by a spectre from beyond the grave bearing a grim message of murder and revenge. The young Prince is driven to the edge of madness by his struggle to understand the situation he finds himself in and to do his duty. Many others, including Hamlet's beloved, the innocent Ophelia, are swept up in his tragedy, Shakespeare's most famous and one of the great stories in the literature of the world.	349	8190
2. **Romeo and Juliet** / Shakespeare, William A stunning performance of Shakespeare's timeless tragedy of young love.	249	6781
3. **Macbeth** / Shakespeare, William Macbeth's ambition unleashes a cycle of violence. Prompted by the supernatural prophecy of three witches, Macbeth kills King Duncan and assumes his throne. Macbeth plunges further into murder and moral decay to keep the crown on his head. While his wife crumbles away in guilt and madness, Macbeth fights to prevent the rest of the prophecy from coming true.	272	6518
4. **Othello** / Shakespeare, William "Othello, a Moorish general in the service of Venice, has married Desdemona, beautiful daughter of a Venetian Senator. But Iago, Othello's malignant ensign, is determined to destroy their happiness"--Container.	178	5566
5. **Julius Caesar** / Shakespeare, William A Shakespeare Society production; a complete play in five acts. Features a unique cover illustration by Maurice Sendak (Where the wild things are), specially commissioned for this work. An introductory essay by Harvard scholar Harold Bloom accompanies this program.	196	4987

Source: Screenshots of OCLC FictionFinder Search results are ©2009 OCLC Online Computer Library Center, Inc. FictionFinder is a trademark and/or service mark of OCLC.

▶ **FIGURE 5-5. The OCLC FictionFinder FRBR View of a Work and Its Expressions and Manifestations**

Hamlet.
Shakespeare, William, 1564-1616

349 editions, in 23 languages, held by 8190 libraries

Summary: Distressed by his father's death and his mother's over-hasty remarriage, Hamlet, Prince of Denmark is faced by a spectre from beyond the grave bearing a grim message of murder and revenge. The young Prince is driven to the edge of madness by his struggle to understand the situation he finds himself in and to do his duty. Many others, including Hamlet's beloved, the innocent Ophelia, are swept up in his tragedy, Shakespeare's most famous and one of the great stories in the literature of the world.

Genres: Tragedies

Characters: Hamlet (Legendary character) | Lear, King (Legendary character)

Settings: Denmark | 1500 - 1600 | 1600 - 1699 | 1400 - 1599 | 1413 - 1422 | 1800 - 1899 | Great Britain | Ohio —Cincinnati [+]

Subjects: Princes | Revenge | Fathers —Death [+] | Murder victims' families | Kings and rulers —Succession [+] | English drama (Tragedy) | Incidental music | Kings and rulers | Monologues | Soliloquy | Advertising | [More]

Audience: ▬▬▬▬▬
Kids   General   Special

Editions	Genres	Characters	Settings	Subjects

Narrow by Languages: All (349)   ▾   Narrow by Format: Show All   ▾

	Title / Author	OCLC #	Date	Language	Format	Aud.	Libraries ▾
1.	Hamlet Shakespeare	55873969	2002	Spanish	eBooks	General	▬▬▬▬
2.	Hamlet by William Shakespeare	08416068	1981	English	Book	General	▬▬▬▬
3.	BBC Radio presents Hamlet William Shakespeare	29500056	1992	English	Book	General	▬▬▬▬
4.	The tragedy of Hamlet, prince of Denmark by William Shakespeare	49293770	199?	English	eBooks	General	▬▬▬▬
5.	Hamlet by William Shakespeare	57028474	1990	English	Book	General	▬▬▬▬
6.	Hamlet William Shakespeare	02880558	1963	English	Book	General	▬▬▬▬

Source: Screenshots of OCLC FictionFinder Search results are ©2009 OCLC Online Computer Library Center, Inc. FictionFinder is a trademark and/or service mark of OCLC.

Libraries Australia FRBR Prototype (LibraryLabs of Libraries Australia)

Developer: National Library of Australia, National Australian Bibliographic Database

URL(s): http://ll01.nla.gov.au

This FRBR-like prototype system is an experimental system based on a copy of the Australian National Bibliographic Database; as of this writing, it mirrors the database as of March 2008 with 16 million records. The prototype was developed to demonstrate an experimental FRBR display of retrieved records. Users are directed to a display with a hyperlink labeled "This title can be viewed as part of an experimental FRBR group" near the top of their search result display page. The FRBR display shows all retrieved records on one page with results clustered by the attributes listed on top, which also serve as local links to support easy navigation within the page. The screen in Figure 5-6 shows a record of *Hamlet* by Shakespeare (a manifestation in this case); the FRBR display hyperlink leads to the screen in Figure 5-7, where records are grouped into separate

▶ FIGURE 5-6. A Record of Shakespeare's *Hamlet* with FRBR Display Hyperlink

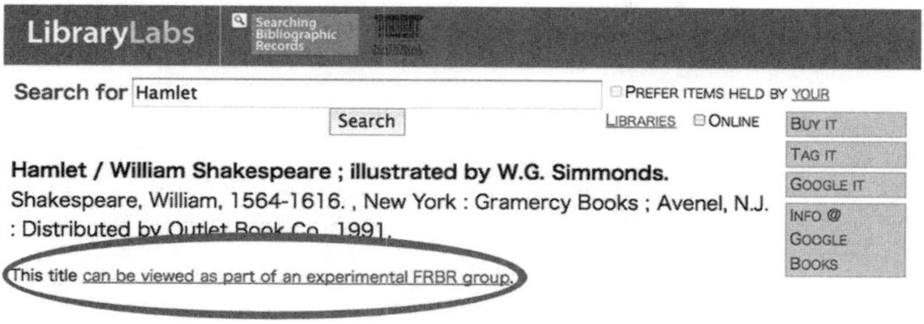
LibraryLabs
Searching Bibliographic Records
Search for Hamlet
Search
PREFER ITEMS HELD BY YOUR LIBRARIES
ONLINE
BUY IT
TAG IT
GOOGLE IT
INFO @ GOOGLE BOOKS
Hamlet / William Shakespeare ; illustrated by W.G. Simmonds.
Shakespeare, William, 1564-1616. , New York : Gramercy Books ; Avenel, N.J. : Distributed by Outlet Book Co. 1991.
This title can be viewed as part of an experimental FRBR group.

Source: National Library of Australia, LibraryLabs, http://ll01.nla.gov.au.

types or forms, such as book, musical score, film, and so on. For records representing materials in book form, there are 31 language expressions, with English being fifth on the language list based on alphabetical order and containing 345 separate editions/publications

▶ FIGURE 5-7. The FRBR-like Display of the Record Clusters for Shakespeare's *Hamlet*

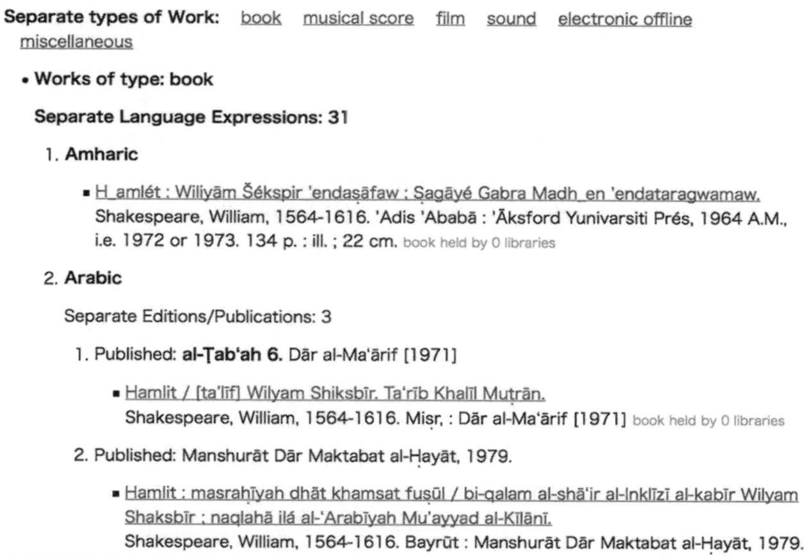
Separate types of Work: book musical score film sound electronic offline miscellaneous
• Works of type: book
Separate Language Expressions: 31
1. Amharic
▪ H_amlét : Wiliyām Šékspir 'endaṣāfaw : Ṣagāyé Gabra Madh_en 'endataragwamaw.
Shakespeare, William, 1564-1616. 'Adis 'Ababā : 'Ăksford Yunivarsiti Prés, 1964 A.M., i.e. 1972 or 1973. 134 p. : ill. ; 22 cm. book held by 0 libraries
2. Arabic
Separate Editions/Publications: 3
1. Published: al-Ṭab'ah 6. Dār al-Ma'ārif [1971]
▪ Hamlit / [ta'līf] Wilyam Shiksbīr. Ta'rīb Khalīl Muṭrān.
Shakespeare, William, 1564-1616. Miṣr, : Dār al-Ma'ārif [1971] book held by 0 libraries
2. Published: Manshurāt Dār Maktabat al-Ḥayāt, 1979.
▪ Hamlit : masraḥīyah dhāt khamsat fuṣūl / bi-qalam al-shā'ir al-Inklīzī al-kabīr Wilyam Shaksbīr ; naqlahā ilá al-'Arabīyah Mu'ayyad al-Kīlānī.
Shakespeare, William, 1564-1616. Bayrūt : Manshurāt Dār Maktabat al-Ḥayāt, 1979.

Source: National Library of Australia, LibraryLabs, http://ll01.nla.gov.au.

▶ FIGURE 5-8. Shakespeare's *Hamlet* in English Books in FRBR Display

5. **English**

Separate Editions/Publications: 345

1. Published: N.S.W. Dept. of Education Div. of Guidance & Special Education.

- The works of William Shakespeare [braille] / edited by William George Clark and William Aldis Wright.
  Shakespeare, William, 1564-1616. North Sydney : N.S.W. Dept. of Education Div. of Guidance & Special Education. 1 v. of interpoint braille. book held by 1 library

2. Published: published by Oliver & Boyd, [n.d.]

- Hamlet : a tragedy, in five acts / By William Shakespeare : As performed at the Theatres-Royal, Drury-Lane and Covent-Garden : Printed under the authority of the managers, from the prompt-books.
  Shakespeare, William, 1564-1616. Edinburgh : published by Oliver & Boyd, [n.d.] 12mo 68 p. ; 15 cm. book held by 1 library

3. Published: Royal Victorian Institute for the Blind Educational Centre.

- Hamlet [braille] / [William Shakespeare].
  Shakespeare, William, 1564-1616. Burwood, Vic. : Royal Victorian Institute for the Blind Educational Centre. 1 v. of interpoint braille. book held by 1 library

4. Published: Shakespeare Head Pr., [n.d.].

- Hamlet.
  Shakespeare, William, 1564-1616. Sydney : Shakespeare Head Pr., [n.d.]. 1 v. book held by 1

Source: National Library of Australia, LibraryLabs, http://ll01.nla.gov.au.

---

listed in the order of year of publication and publisher, as shown in Figure 5-8. The developers of this prototype call this display "FRBR-like" because its display does not strictly follow the hierarchal structure of the Group 1 entities. Instead, the display mixes FRBR expressions and manifestations by grouping retrieved results first by format (which they refer to as "type of work"), next by language, and then by edition and publication details. They argue that this is a useful approach when people look for materials in a specific form and language.

RedLightGreen

Developer: Research Libraries Group (now part of OCLC)

URL(s): No longer available

RedLightGreen was an online union catalog designed specifically as an intuitive online research tool for undergraduate students. It is one of the first FRBR-based systems widely cited in early literature and presentations about FRBR implementations. RedLightGreen is no longer available as its role has largely been taken over by WorldCat.org. RedLightGreen adopted some FRBR concepts, but it was not a full FRBR implementation. Its project developers described this prototype as a FRBRish, not FRBRized, catalog that utilized many of the intellectual concepts behind FRBR in its design such as using work, expression, manifestation, and item to cluster records in the catalog (Proffitt, 2004). Specifically, RedLightGreen used both work and expression to correspond to the "title clusters," manifestation to correspond to specific editions, and items to correspond to items.

BIBSYS
Developer: Norwegian National Library, Norwegian University of Science and Technology, Library of Norway
URL(s): www.bibsys.no (the full system); http://november.idi.ntnu.no/frbrized (prototype system; not currently accessible)
BIBSYS supplies library and information systems to over 100 Norwegian libraries and institutions of higher education, including university libraries, a number of research institutions, and the Norwegian National Library. The goal of the BIBSYS FRBR project is to investigate the possibilities and techniques for applying the FRBR model to preexisting MARC databases. Records of the BIBSYS bibliographic database have been successfully FRBRized through the development of an XML-based tool that extracts relevant FRBR entity information from MARC records. The project also produced a software tool that can automatically interpret and extract existing MARC record information based on the FRBR model and can therefore be used to FRBRize a MARC-based bibliographic catalog. Since some documents about the project's technical details are written in Norwegian and the prototype system is not currently accessible, some of the system's FRBR features cannot be illustrated here. It is unclear whether the full BIBSYS catalog contains any FRBR features.

Kent State University FRBR Project
Developer: Kent State University School of Library and Information Science
URL(s): http://frbr.slis.kent.edu
The Kent State FRBR project aims to survey, examine, and compare FRBR-related research and practice to reveal the current status of

the field, including major developments, problems, and issues. In particular, this project examines and evaluates existing FRBR prototypes and models from the end user's perspective. One of the project's goals is to develop a FRBR-based catalog to effectively support user tasks and to facilitate information seeking. The system will be built based on user studies of existing FRBR-based systems and prototypes as well as direct user input and user evaluations during the process of system design and development. The collection for the system is a December 31, 2007 download of Library of Congress records from OCLC WorldCat that contains over 13.5 million bibliographic records and over 7 million authority records. The project adopts an open source approach for the FRBR system development and has identified Koha as a base system upon which to build the FRBR system. The project is still ongoing and is expected to be completed by September of 2010.

Algorithms and Software for FRBR Implementation

Software for Building Catalogs and Other Systems

eXtensible Catalog (XC)

Developer: The University of Rochester's River Campus Libraries
URL(s): www.extensiblecatalog.info
eXtensible Catalog (XC) is an ongoing project to develop a set of open source software tools for building online systems that can provide unified access to traditional and digital library resources. Among many other features, it will support FRBRization of metadata that reflect the emerging technologies and standards for libraries, such as using Open Archives Initiative Protocol for Metadata Harvesting (OAI PMH) to aggregate metadata from a variety of sources, transforming and crosswalking various metadata created in different schemas, enabling a faceted user interface, embedding Application Programming Interface (API) in its XC software to support easy development of additional services, and facilitating future adoption of the Resource Description and Access (RDA) standard. It is noted that FRBRization in XC focuses on Group 1 entities in the FRBR model instead of a full implementation. The project has been developed with a strong

user focus supported by previous usability test results and new user studies of students and faculty in four universities exploring how they find and acquire research materials from traditional library sources and other physical and digital collections. The project released a major white paper about its metadata approach in early January 2009 (Bowen, 2009) and plans to release the XC software in late July 2009.

Virtua ILS (Integrated Library Systems)
Developer: VTLS (Visionary Technology in Library Solutions)
URL(s): www.vtls.com/products/virtua

In Virtua, VTLS has attempted to create an environment in which records following the FRBR model can coexist with records in traditional cataloging models. The software is "FRBR aware" and automatically switches display formats depending on the type of record accessed. Its FRBR display supports a hierarchical view of work, expression, and manifestation in an expandable tree structure according to music, sound recording, language material, etc. It also supports viewing the FRBR hierarchy in reverse order from manifestation to expression to work. As demonstrated in exhibitions at both the 2008 ALA (American Library Association) Annual Conference and the 2009 ALA Mid-winter Meeting, VTLS also offers a Software as a Service (SaaS) option for the FRBR display that can be linked from a library's catalog to a VTLS server, and from there users can switch back to the regular catalog display at the library. This implementation allows libraries to take advantage of the FRBR model without massive local efforts.

Innovative Interfaces
Developer: Innovative Interfaces, Inc. (III)
URL(s): www.iii.com

Innovative Interfaces has investigated the potential integration of FRBR into their line of products, specifically the Millennium ILS, to enable systems to return structured search results of works available in many different versions, formats, and languages. However, further development and product release is on hold pending the release of the RDA standard.

VisualCat

Developer: Portia

URL(s): www.portia.dk/websites/productgallery.htm

VisualCat is a cataloging software system developed and distributed by Portia. It has been developed as an integrated solution for copy cataloging and bibliographic metadata management within a single framework based on RDF (Resource Description Framework) and FRBR. It can be used to develop a cataloging client or integrated library system that is capable of serving an accurate, user-friendly catalog. However, no new information about the product has been available at its main Web site since 2005.

OpenFRBR

Developer: William Denton

URL(s): www.openfrbr.org

OpenFRBR is an open source software tool for FRBR implementation of "everything." It considers FRBR entities, relationships, and user tasks of equal importance (Denton, 2006). The most recent version, OpenFRBR 2.1, can perform a partial implementation of FRBR with Group 1, Group 2, and Group 3 entities and with some of the relationships among the entities. The project site offers a demonstration of how the software may work using the *Harry Potter* bibliographic universe as the testing data set. The demonstration site allows users to edit and play with the data elements by adding, deleting, connecting, and establishing attributes, entities, and relationships in the given data set. The project is still evolving with an expected expansion of the implementation to include more relationships between entities (e.g., the relationship between work and expression) and to address character set issues.

IFPA (ISIS FRBR Prototype Application)

Developer: Roberto Sturman, University of Trieste

URL(s): http://pclib3.ts.infn.it/frbr/wwwisis/FRB2.01/FORM.HTM

IFPA (ISIS FRBR Prototype Application) is an experimental FRBR tool developed to manage data and relationships according to the FRBR model, and it serves as an application for the UNESCO

ISIS retrieval software. Its latest version, IFPA2, was released in July 2008. The new version is based on a heavily modified version of the WEBLIS integrated library system that now supports a graphical interface for data entry and allows creation of an unlimited number of relationships among the FRBR entities. IFPA2 can also manage FRBR entities, their attributes, and entity relationships. The tool's developer stresses that the tool is meant to serve as an academic experiment that will assist people interested in implementing the FRBR model (Sturman, 2005). An online demonstration is available at the project Web site to show the examples included in the IFLA's (International Federation of Library Associations and Institutions) *FRBR Final Report* and to illustrate its implementation approach.

LibDB
Developer: Morbus
URL(s): http://sourceforge.net/projects/libdb
LibDB is open source software for library and asset management inspired by FRBR, RDF triples, and end usability. It supports cataloging of all types of resources, such as movies, books, comics, and serials. SourceForge.net has a registered entry for this software (http://sourceforge.net/projects/libdb) with version 0.0.3 available for download, but the project has not been under active development since December 18, 2007.

FRBRization Algorithms and Tools

OCLC FRBR Work-Set Algorithm
Developer: OCLC
URL(s): www.oclc.org/research/projects/frbr/algorithm.htm
The OCLC FRBR Work-Set Algorithm was developed to examine the issues associated with the automatic FRBRization process and serve as a basis for implementing FRBR prototype systems on a large scale. The algorithm uses both authority records and bibliographic records to cluster catalog records at the work level. The algorithm has been used in many FRBR system development projects, including OCLC FictionFinder and WorldCat.org. The Libraries Australia's FRBR prototype system and Kent State

University's FRBR project have adapted the algorithm for their respective FRBR implementations. The OCLC FRBR Work-Set Algorithm is not a software program that is ready to use. It is up to software developers to implement the algorithm using a chosen programming language.

Tool for Converting Bibliographic Records

Developer: Norwegian National Library, Norwegian University of Science and Technology, Library of Norway

URL(s): www.ercim.org/publication/Ercim_News/enw66/aalberg.html

This conversion tool, developed as part of the BIBSYS project, can perform an automatic interpretation and conversion of existing information within MARC records into a format that directly reflects the FRBR model. The major difference between this tool and others is that it can support the full conversion of data in MARC records to reflect the FRBR entities, attributes, and relationships. Although some information (e.g., a person's name or a work title) may appear multiple times in numerous records, the final output of the FRBRization process "should be a normalized set of unique entities with a proper set of attributes and relationships" (Aalberg, 2006: 1). SourceForge.net, a source code repository for open source software, has a registered entry for this tool (http://sourceforge.net/projects/marc2frbr), but the information has not been updated in two years.

Display Tools

FRBR Display Tool

Developer: Network Development and MARC Standards Office, Library of Congress

URL(s): www.loc.gov/marc/marc-functional-analysis/tool.html

Currently at Version 2.0, the FRBR Display Tool is a freely downloadable tool that analyzes MARC data through the work, expression, manifestation, and item entities of the FRBR model and creates FRBR displays accordingly. The MARC data can be a retrieved file of MARC records from systems such as online library catalogs. This tool allows libraries to experiment with FRBR without changing catalog records but still provides library users with better collocating and sorting of retrieved records by grouping them into the work, expression, and manifestation **FRBR** entities. This tool has been used by several research experiments, and more discussion is available later in this chapter in the section on utilization and evaluation of current algorithms and software for FRBR implementations.

FRBR Floater

Developer: Monte Sano Associates

URL(s): www.montesanoassociates.com/apps-msafrbr.htm

FRBR Floater is a subscription service that enables users to view, via a pop-up OPAC window, various editions and formats of items in a particular library given any title searched if the search results in more than one edition or format. It will help library users browse a structured list and identify and select one item. With this tool, libraries do not need to make changes to their existing records because the provider uses an algorithm to extract data from a library's existing MARC catalog records for the display based on the FRBR model.

OVERVIEW OF FRBR IMPLEMENTATION PROJECTS

This section summarizes the current FRBR implementation projects in terms of some key implementation considerations. Specifically, the implementation efforts and approaches are reviewed and discussed in the following areas: (1) purpose, (2) FRBR model focus, (3) system collection, (4) record creation and FRBRization, (5) system user interface and display, (6) system architecture and other technical details, and (7) user evaluation and testing.

Purpose

In line with the goal of FRBR itself to facilitate user tasks, the goal of all recently developed FRBR-related projects is to provide users with a quick and effective method of fulfilling their informational needs. FRBR entities are meant to provide fewer but more relevant search results and to present and rank these results via various means in a way that is understandable to the user. Additional goals for the FRBR projects include the following:

> ▶ Allowing users to access information via union catalogs

> ▶ Serving the needs of specialized settings and collections and their respective user needs

> ▶ Economically FRBRizing legacy data (especially existing MARC records)

> ▶ Integrating bibliographic data with a variety of other data sources

> ▶ Developing algorithms and software to facilitate FRBRization of data, creation of FRBR-friendly records, and storage and management of records.

FRBR Model Focus

Overall, the goal of most FRBR projects surveyed is the implementation of the FRBR model to organize their collection based on the Group 1 entities: work, expression, manifestation, and item. Many projects modify the representation of entities into a different grouping of records or results display. For example:

> ▶ OCLC FictionFinder, a collection of fiction, presents results as lists of works. Expressions of a work are then organized by language.

> ▶ WorldCat.org uses a FRBR-like approach to cluster results for works, expressions, and manifestations.

> ▶ RedLightGreen collapsed FRBR's four levels into just two, displaying a work and various manifestations of that work.

> ▶ Libraries Australia FRBR prototype introduced an additional entity, the superwork, for entities represented by more than one work.

The BIBSYS project might be the most comprehensive implementation of the FRBR model. OpenFRBR also includes FRBR entities beyond Group 1, although the relationships among the entities have not been fully included. In the case of library consortia, item-level information is often omitted with the reasoning that individual library catalogs provide such access on their own. Catalogs of individual institutions are more likely to represent item-level records.

System Collection

The size and nature of collections in FRBR-related projects and prototypes vary. Consortia are the predominant form among the major FRBR implementations. Implementations based on their collections can take the form of

- ▶ international consortia (WorldCat.org, RedLightGreen),
- ▶ international union catalogs for a specific genre (OCLC FictionFinder),
- ▶ national consortia and databases (BIBSYS, Libraries Australia), and
- ▶ individual library or archive collections (UCLA Film and Television Archive).

Some projects are ILS applications to be used by libraries and, therefore, do not have their own collections. For these, like VisualCat and Virtua ILS, the collection coverage depends on the library using the system. It is interesting to note that while some projects involve general library collections, others are developed for specific collections. For example, the UCLA Film and Television Archive OPAC embodied the FRBR principles with a particular application in retrieving moving images. OCLC FictionFinder was developed to search works of fiction with search and browsing features and options that make use of characteristics specific to fiction using options such as literary award winners, genre (e.g., adventure fiction, love stories, science fiction, spy stories, etc.), fictional characters, and setting. In addition, some projects such as eXtensible Catalog and WorldCat may allow and support data beyond traditional bibliographic records to provide integrated access and display of a variety of data sources under the FRBR framework.

Record Creation and FRBRization

Just as the FRBR focus varies among implementations, the means for record creation and FRBRization also vary. Large-scale projects, such as WorldCat, RedLightGreen, BIBSYS, and Libraries Australia, have adopted and/or developed various algorithms to support their respective goals:

▶ WorldCat.org and FictionFinder utilized the OCLC Work-Set Algorithm to develop clusters of works, expressions, and manifestations.

▶ The UCLA project applies the FRBR model when cataloging within a traditional ILS/catalog system.

▶ Libraries Australia's algorithm, drawn in part from the Library of Congress FRBR Display Tool and the OCLC Work-Set Algorithm, was designed with display as its primary goal.

▶ BIBSYS used XSLT (eXtensible Stylesheet Language Transformations) and MarcXchange in an algorithm that FRBRizes records from any MARC format/cataloging standard.

▶ Software vendors, such as VTLS, have implemented some aspects of on-demand FRBRization for individual library collections in their systems but keep FRBR records alongside traditional MARC records.

Some projects were developed mainly to FRBRize legacy data, such as MARC record data. The most widely used FRBRization algorithm so far is the OCLC FRBR Work-Set Algorithm, which has been utilized in most of the large-scale projects, such as WorldCat.org, FictionFinder, and Libraries Australia. It is noted that the versatility and interoperability potential of XML has made it a popular base for FRBRization projects. For example, RedLightGreen developed its own XML DTD (Document Type Definition) for MARC records, which forms title clusters pointing to editions, translations, and adaptations.

Interface and Display

For users to interact with available systems during their information-seeking process, a system interface is essential. The FRBR model, with its focus on user tasks, offers great potential for developing effective and user-friendly system interfaces and displays. A number of interface and display structures are inherent in recent and ongoing FRBR implementation projects. Among the more popular is the hierarchical "tree" structure that allows a user to navigate from works to expressions to manifestations.

Some commonly available features, both FRBR-based and non-FRBR-specific, include the following:

▶ Retrieved results display as a list of works rather than as a list of individual bibliographic records (FictionFinder).

▶ Availability of the FRBR hierarchy is preserved throughout the search process (BIBSYS).

▶ Faceted displays enable a user to narrow results by various criteria, such as subject, genre, edition, date, and language (WorldCat.org, FictionFinder, and Libraries Australia FRBR prototype).

▶ Support for multiple interface languages and an option for switching the interface display to any one of six major world languages is available (WorldCat.org).

▶ Multiple search methods, including keyword search, wild card search, complex Boolean search, cross index search with index specification, and special limited searches are offered (UCLA).

▶ A popular automatic bibliographic citation feature is used (RedLightGreen and WorldCat.org).

Notably, some projects were developed mainly to support FRBR display and can work on top of existing online library catalogs. This offers great opportunities for libraries to have a FRBRized look for their catalogs without significant investment or major system changes because some tools, such as the FRBR Display Tool developed by the Network Development and MARC Standards Office at the Library of Congress, are freely available for download. The FRBR display tools also offer great opportunities for researchers and developers to reconfigure different interface and display options with relatively minor development efforts in the process of exploring more effective user interfaces.

System Architecture and Other Technical Details

Very few FRBR projects make available their system implementation details, such as system architecture and functional components, software and hardware, and other technical specifics. The related information available in the public domain largely concerns system development process details and procedures. While full-scale systems tend to have close ties with their traditional counterparts' system structure in order to provide full services (e.g., UCLA Film and Television Archive OPAC is built upon Voyager ILS), FRBR prototypes or experimental test systems are more flexible and tend to have their own system implementation approaches. For example,

▶ FictionFinder used the Work-Set Algorithm to extract elements from existing records to form a key that is used as a basis for grouping existing records. It also uses OCLC-developed NACO (Name Authority Cooperative Program) authority normalization rules to simplify names and titles.

▶ RedLightGreen developed its own XML DTD for MARC records—an iterative process that required modification of the initial Library of Congress DTD, testing with sample data, and then additional modification.

▶ BIBSYS developed its own conversion tool through the use of XSLT (the W3C language for transforming XML for record conversion and follow-up record processing).

It is interesting to note that many algorithms and software developed for the FRBR catalog systems and prototypes are now freely available for further FRBR development (e.g., the Work-Set Algorithm developed for FictionFinder and the conversion tool developed as part of the BIBSYS project). Some software for FRBR implementations that is now freely available includes the Library of Congress FRBR Display Tool, the IFPA-ISIS FRBR Prototype Application, and LibDB. Such resources offer great opportunities for future FRBR system development.

User Evaluation and Testing

As part of the ongoing process of reviewing current FRBR implementation projects, the authors of this book surveyed the various project leaders in March 2007 to ask follow-up questions and request additional project-specific information not available at individual project Web sites or in the project-related publications. The survey results revealed that most projects had not included or reported user studies on their FRBR developments. However, many project leaders indicated that they either planned to conduct user studies in the future or had the desire but not the resources to do so. This lack of user perspective in FRBR research and development will be discussed in Chapter 6.

CRITICAL ISSUES AND CHALLENGES IN FRBR IMPLEMENTATIONS

At this early stage of FRBR implementation, it is beneficial to identify and discuss the related issues and challenges. This section first reviews FRBR implementation issues and challenges covered in the associated literature and then reports on the key issues and challenges as identified from the FRBR Delphi study for future implementations.

Issues and Challenges Covered in Literature

FRBRization of Legacy Data

FRBRization of existing online library catalogs has been one of the major discussion topics addressed in FRBR-related literature. Presently, it is challenging to trace and extract FRBR data elements and record structures from existing MARC records in current library catalogs. Some of the reasons cited include the following:

▶ Some records contain incorrect information due to cataloging errors (Zhang and Salaba, 2009; Hegna and Murtomaa, 2003).

▶ MARC records are based on current cataloging rules and practices that do not readily fit the FRBR model. Some records do not contain the information needed to construct FRBR data. For example, expressions and manifestations are typically not distinguished in current cataloging practice, and many bibliographic records do not contain enough expression-level information (Hegna and Murtomaa, 2003; O'Neill, 2002).

► Some collocating information is recorded in a way that is hard for computers to trace and process. In particular, inconsistent treatment of key collocating information based on current cataloging practice (e.g., contributors to a given work are recorded in various fields [245 $c, 700, 500, and 250]) makes it difficult to automatically collocate expressions (Ercegovac, 2006; Hegna and Murtomaa, 2003).

Based on their FRBRization experiment of the Library of Congress collection using the OCLC FRBR Work-Set Algorithm, Zhang and Salaba (2009) group the FRBRization issues and challenges into two categories: (1) algorithm related, and (2) legacy data and current cataloging practices and standards related. While there is room to refine the algorithm to address some of the issues and challenges, often developing a common rule for blanket automatic processing may come with trade-offs and compromises due to the errors and abnormalities in legacy data.

There have been efforts to address these issues and challenges. The Library of Congress's Network Development and MARC Standards Office (NDMSO) has commissioned a study to examine MARC21 from several perspectives, including FRBR, and recommended ways of mapping MARC data elements to FRBR (Network Development and MARC Standards Office, 2006). One purpose of the study was to explore and recommend ways to create records that describe and display multiple manifestations of the same work and support the display of hierarchical relationships among records (Network Development and MARC Standards Office, 2006). This NDMSO study will contribute to the FRBRization of library catalogs that are largely based on MARC records. In a review of problems users encounter when searching for known works in current OPACs, Martha Yee (2005) indicated that a better understanding of AACR2 (*Anglo-American Cataloguing Rules*, Second Edition)/ MARC21 authority, bibliographic, and holdings records would help to address problems in FRBRizing current OPACs using existing records. Yee discussed and provided examples of work identifiers and expression identifiers in both bibliographic and authority records. After Yee surveyed and reviewed several FRBR implementation projects, she suggested possible ways to improve the implementations to address the problems users are facing.

Identification and Presentation of Bibliographic Relationships

A challenging and much debated aspect of FRBR implementation, also a weak area in current FRBR implementation projects, is the identification and presentation of bibliographic relationships to facilitate user searching, browsing, and collocating (Riva, 2004). However, some bibliographic relationships such as derivative relationships are not implemented in currently operational OPACs (Hegna and Murtomaa, 2003). There has been a call for mechanisms that guide users in browsing and searching resources that are linked together by explicitly expressed relationships (Ercegovac, 2006).

Utilization and Evaluation of Implementation Software Tools and Algorithms

Because the software tools and algorithms are developed largely for automatic processing, it is important to know how well they are constructed and how efficiently they function in achieving the goals for which they are designed. However, there has been a shortage of such evaluative work. For example, as noted by Carlyle, Ranger, and Sumlnerlin (2008), the OCLC FRBR Work-Set Algorithm has been commonly used in many FRBR system development projects; however, there have not been investigations into its effectiveness. Such work is valuable not only in improving the algorithm but also in finding alternative approaches to FRBR implementation.

There have been various software tools and algorithms developed that are freely available, some of which perform similar functions. The differences and limitations of these tools and algorithms need to be better understood so that they can be better utilized. For example, it is recognized that the conversion tool for BIBSYS can be applied to convert MARC bibliographic records to FRBR entities at all levels, while the OCLC algorithm is known to perform well in identifying FRBR works yet has various limitations in identifying entities beyond works (Aalberg, Haugen, and

Husby, 2006; Hickey, O'Neill, and Toves, 2002; O'Neill, 2002). Still, there has not been robust testing of the conversion tool for BIBSYS on a large number of records to evaluate its scalability and to uncover various cases for selecting and assigning MARC fields to different entities in order to establish the relationships between these entities. So far, the tool has been used to convert 4,000,000 records in the BIBSYS bibliographic database. The developers did caution that, at this stage, a full conversion to a FRBR-based data model may not be realistic or desirable for most libraries due to limited knowledge about the application aspect of the model and the lack of standardized formats for FRBR (Aalberg, Haugen, and Husby, 2006). This view was shared by the OCLC Work-Set Algorithm team, whose experimental results support this opinion and justify their development focus on work level FRBRization (Hickey, O'Neill, and Toves, 2002; O'Neill, 2002).

The FRBR Display Tool offers libraries great opportunities to easily experiment with the FRBRization of their library catalogs. It has been used for FRBRization experiments (Schneider, 2008) as well as for user studies on various displays and interfaces (Ercegovac, 2006; Kilner, 2005; Rajapatirana and Missingham, 2005). Like other tools that utilize MARC records, the effectiveness and usefulness of the FRBR Display Tool relies, to a great extent, on the quality of data in existing MARC records. Errors and data inconsistency in bibliographic records will lessen the utility of the display. As reported in the project Web site, the tool has some limitations in performance: it works best with record sets resulting from searches of name and title fields and broader searches. Some additional issues and limitations were reported based on experimentations and evaluations of the tool:

▶ The tool performs an XML conversion; this could be problematic for implementations where locally defined MARC tags must be incorporated into standard XML DTD (Rajapatirana and Missingham, 2005).

▶ It is very sensitive to data errors within Australia National Bibliographic Database records, particularly in the transformation from MARC to XML (Rajapatirana and Missingham, 2005).

▶ It does not generate statistics on completion of processing (Rajapatirana and Missingham, 2005).

▶ The algorithm does not differentiate between musical and nonmusical sound recordings for display purposes (Rajapatirana and Missingham, 2005).

▶ The displays are sometimes confusing and misleading due to sorting rules and criteria imposed by the tool (Rajapatirana and Missingham, 2005; Yee, 2005).

▶ It omits fairly vital information because it does not display summary holdings (Rajapatirana and Missingham, 2005).

▶ It assumes that only bibliographic records will be searched and displayed; authority records cannot be used (Yee, 2005).

▶ The FRBR display tool document seems to imply that only language change discriminates expressions and that all other changes (such as edition statement changes and changes in subsidiary authorship) are manifestation changes (Yee, 2005).

Plans for improvements of the tool are in place, including extending the matching, sorting, and displaying of results to analytical headings from added entry fields in 7xx; displaying the MARC field that contains the matching data in the display module; and creating a Web application functionally comparable to the current local computer application (Radebaugh and Keith, 2005).

It was noted that some software tools and algorithms were developed for a particular system, project, or data set. Besides the need for testing the tools and algorithms against large data sets, more research and evaluation would be beneficial in comparing their performances. Suggested tests include a performance comparison among similar tools and algorithms as well as a performance evaluation of automatic and manual processing to improve effectiveness.

Implementation Guidelines

A key challenge for FRBR implementations is the transformation of the conceptual model into clear implementation guidelines.

There have been concerns that, as a conceptual model, FRBR could lead to different implementations and various interpretations due to the lack of detailed cataloging rules based on the model (Carlyle, 2006). This challenge has been commonly reported in essentially all types of FRBR implementation projects and research. Specific guidelines are needed for some key implementation questions: how to identify FRBR entities from existing bibliographic records, how to draw precise boundaries among the four FRBR entities, how to establish relationships among FRBR entities, and how to display FRBR entities, relationships, and attributes. Among the FRBR entities, some success has been reported from implementations related to work entities, while difficulties have been reported from implementations related to manifestation and expression entities and relationships (e.g., Ercegovac, 2006; Hickey and O'Neill, 2005; Bennett, Lavoie, and O'Neill, 2003; Monch and Aalberg, 2003; O'Neill, 2002; Hickey, O'Neill, and Toves, 2002).

Collocation

Current library catalogs do not effectively divulge pertinent information on related materials. The emphasis on user tasks and hierarchical relationships in FRBR offers opportunities to enhance user experiences with search displays and locating and collocating associated materials. Research has shown that by assembling bibliographic records into interrelated clusters and displaying the hierarchy and relationships based on the FRBR model, a new navigational capability in networked digital libraries can be developed (Ercegovac, 2006). However, current cataloging practice and existing cataloging data hinder the creation of such hierarchical displays. For example, it is difficult to group manifestations into expressions, to display those expressions under a given work, and to indicate other related works (Ercegovac, 2006). The research further calls for more work to exploit available information from MARC records that would be useful for facilitating user decision-making during browsing and searching.

What complicates the matter is that any solution to address the issue may involve possible revisions of cataloging rules and approaches in order to realize collocating in catalogs, as evidenced by the deliberation on single record versus separate records options, concerns about the practicality of expression-level cataloging versus manifestation-level cataloging, and considerations regarding the ability to maintain consistency and continuity with the legacy of bibliographic records (Oliver, 2004).

Interoperability

FRBRization of existing data and records requires dealing with bibliographic records and other types of records, such as authority records. Interoperability has been raised as an important issue in the process of matching and comparing records across files and systems. Researchers have identified the essential role of normalization of records from different systems in FRBR implementations and have explored ways to improve current practices and rules (Hickey, Toves, and O'Neill, 2006). Interoperability issues have also been explored at the metadata schema level (Chen and Chen, 2004). As library catalogs move toward the Web-based integrated environment, interoperability will become a more critical and pressing issue, as only this will allow library users to search all potential sources of information (Gradmann, 2005; Tillett, 2005).

Issues and Challenges as Identified in the Delphi Study

The FRBR Delphi panel raised ten of the most critical issues related to FRBR implementations (see Chapter 1). These are summarized below in the order of their importance, as determined by the panel members:

▶ Issue 1: Need to develop and test tools/software that will facilitate the FRBRization processes.

▶ Issue 2: Need to explore, develop, and test various means of FRBR implementation.

▶ Issue 3: Need to address the FRBRization of existing data from a variety of differing standards and practices.

▶ Issue 4: Need to explore, design, and develop effective user interfaces in general, with result displays, in particular, based on the FRBR model.

▶ Issue 5: Need applicable implementation models (in contrast to the conceptual model) to facilitate the development of FRBR-based systems.

▶ Issue 6: Need to develop new full-scale FRBR systems that are not dependent on older practices.

▶ Issue 7: Need to address the FRBRization of existing systems.

▶ Issue 8: Need to explore and address FRBRization issues in general.

▶ Issue 9: Need to develop common systems usable by all parties involved such as publishers, archives, museums, and libraries, etc.

▶ Issue 10: Need to develop FRBR-based systems for consortial situations.

Not surprisingly, these issues have largely been covered in current literature and discussed in the previous section. The order of ranking shows a group consensus on the importance and urgency of these issues to be addressed for future FRBR implementations.

SUMMARY

While the current FRBR-related implementation efforts are largely exploratory in nature, they have, nevertheless, provided a great starting point for further development. User involvement in FRBR implementation and evaluation has not been explored at this stage. Current development efforts largely reflect the points of view of researchers, developers, and librarians on behalf of users rather than the opinions of users themselves. The major issues and challenges facing FRBR implementation for online library catalogs include developing and testing tools and software to facilitate the FRBRization of existing data and systems, exploring various means for FRBR implementation at this early stage of FRBR system development, developing FRBR implementation guidelines, and creating user interfaces that effectively support user tasks. The most challenging aspect of FRBR implementation is probably the lack of internationally agreed on FRBR-related standards for cataloging, record structures, and record encoding, as well as the lack of general frameworks for overall FRBR development.

REFERENCES

Aalberg, Trond. 2006. "A Tool for Converting Bibliographic Records." Available: www.ercim.org/publication/Ercim_News/enw66/aalberg .html (accessed July 30, 2009).

Aalberg, Trond, Frank B. Haugen, and Ole Husby. 2006. "A Tool for Converting from MARC to FRBR." In *Lecture Notes in Computer Science: Vol. 4172. Research and Advanced Technology for Digital Libraries* (pp. 453–456), edited by Julio Gonzalo et al. Berlin: Springer.

Bennett, Rick, Brian F. Lavoie, and Edward T. O'Neill. 2003. "The Concept of a Work in WorldCat: An Application of FRBR." *Library Collections Acquisitions and Technical Services* 27, no. 1: 45–59.

Bowen, Jennifer. 2009. *Supporting the eXtensible Catalog through Metadata Design and Services.* Available: www.extensiblecatalog.org/Metadata Reports (accessed July 30, 2009).

Carlyle, Allyson. 2006. "Understanding FRBR as a Conceptual Model: FRBR and the Bibliographic Universe." *Library Resources and Technical Services* 50, no. 4: 264–273.

Carlyle, Allyson, Sara Ranger, and Joel Sumlnerlin. 2008. "Making the Pieces Fit: *Little Women,* Works, and the Pursuit of Quality." *Cataloging & Classification Quarterly* 46, no. 1: 35–63.

Chen, Yaning, and Shu-jiun Chen. 2004. "A Metadata Practice of the IFLA FRBR Model: A Case Study for the National Palace Museum in Taipei." *Journal of Documentation* 60, no. 2: 128–143.

Denton, William. 2006. *OpenFRBR Manifesto Number One.* Available: www.frbr.org/2006/11/01/openfrbr-manifesto (accessed July 30, 2009).

Ercegovac, Zorana. 2006. "Multiple-Version Resources in Digital Libraries: Towards User-Centered Displays." *Journal of the American Society for Information Science and Technology* 57, no. 8: 1023–1032.

Gradmann, Stefan. 2005. "RDFS: FRBR—Towards an Implementation Model for Library Catalogs Using Semantic Web Technology." *Cataloging & Classification Quarterly* 39, no. 3/4: 63–75.

Hegna, Knut, and Eeva Murtomaa. 2003. "Data Mining MARC to Find: FRBR?" *International Cataloguing and Bibliographic Control: Quarterly Bulletin of the IFLA UBCIM Programme* 32, no. 3: 52–55.

Hickey, Thomas B., and Edward T. O'Neill. 2005. "FRBRizing OCLC's WorldCat." *Cataloging & Classification Quarterly* 39, no. 3/4: 239–251.

Hickey, Thomas B., Edward T. O'Neill, and Jenny Toves. 2002. "Experiments with the IFLA Functional Requirements for Bibliographic Records (FRBR)." *D-Lib Magazine* 8, no. 9. Available: www.dlib.org/dlib/september02/hickey/09hickey.html (accessed July 30, 2009).

Hickey, Thomas B., Jenny Toves, and Edward T. O'Neill. 2006. "NACO Normalization: A Detailed Examination of the Authority File Comparison Rules." *Library Resources and Technical Services* 50, no. 3: 166–172.

Kilner, Kerry. 2005. "The AustLit Gateway and Scholarly Bibliography: A Specialist Implementation of the FRBR." *Cataloging & Classification Quarterly* 39, no. 3/4: 87–102.

Monch, Christian, and Trond Aalberg. 2003. "Automatic Conversion from MARC to FRBR." In *Research and Advanced Technology for Digital Libraries* (pp. 405–411), edited by Traugott Koch and Ingeborg Torvik Sølvberg. Berlin: Springer. Available: www.springerlink.com/content/gfj2rrqrev0tj94t/fulltext.pdf (accessed July 30, 2009).

Network Development and MARC Standards Office. 2006. *Functional Analysis of the MARC 21 Bibliographic and Holdings Formats.* Washington, DC: Library of Congress. Available: www.loc.gov/marc/marc-functional-analysis/functional-analysis.html (accessed July 30, 2009).

O'Neill, Edward T. 2002. "FRBR: Functional Requirements for Bibliographic Records: Application of the Entity-relationship Model to Humphry Clinker." *Library Resources and Technical Services* 46, no. 4: 150–159.

Oliver, Chris. 2004. "FRBR Is Everywhere, but What Happened to the Format Variation Issue? Content Versus Carrier in FRBR." *The Serials Librarian* 45, no. 4: 27–36.

Proffitt, Merrilee. 2004. "RedLightGreen–FRBR between a Rock and a Hard Place." A presentation at ALCTS Preconference, 2005 ALA Annual Meeting. Available: www.wla.lib.wi.us/conferences/2004/postconf/Proffitt.ppt (accessed July 30, 2009).

Radebaugh, Jacqueline, and Corey Keith. 2005. "FRBR Display Tool." *Cataloging & Classification Quarterly* 39, no. 3/4: 271–283.

Rajapatirana, Bemal, and Roxanne Missingham. 2005. "The Australian National Bibliographic Database and the Functional Requirements for the Bibliographic Database (FRBR)." *The Australian Library Journal* 54, no. 1: 31–42.

Riva, Pat. 2004. "Mapping MARC 21 Linking Entry Fields to FRBR and Tillett's Taxonomy of Bibliographic Relationships." *Library Resources and Technical Services* 48, no. 2: 130–143.

Schneider, Jodi. 2008. "FRBRizing MARC Records with the FRBR Display Tool." Available: www.neasist.org/awards/schneider2008.pdf (accessed July 30, 2009).

Sturman, Roberto. 2005. "Implementing the FRBR Conceptual Approach in the ISIS Software Environment: IFPA (ISIS FRBR Prototype Application)." *Cataloging & Classification Quarterly* 39, no. 3/4: 253–270.

Tillett, Barbara. B. 2005. "FRBR and Cataloging for the Future." *Cataloging & Classification Quarterly* 39, no. 3/4: 197–205.

Yee, Martha M. 2005. "FRBRization: A Method for Turning Online Public Finding Lists into Online Public Catalogs." *Information Technology and Libraries* 24, no. 2: 77–95.

Yee, Martha M. 2007. "A FRBR Based Catalog for Moving Images." Available: www.frbr.org/2007/02/07/ucla (accessed July 30, 2009).

Zhang, Yin, and Athena Salaba. 2009. "FRBRizing Legacy Data: Issues and Challenges." ALA 2009 Midwinter Conference, ALA ALCTS CCS Cataloging Norms Interest Group (January 23–28). Available: http://frbr.slis.kent.edu/presentations/ALA2009-midwinter-Norm.pdf (accessed July 30, 2009).

FRBR RESEARCH

The major FRBR (Functional Requirements for Bibliographic Records) developments are reflected in the areas of (1) the FRBR model, background, and theory; (2) FRBR and related standards; (3) FRBR application; (4) FRBR implementation; and (5) FRBR research. Chapters 2, 3, 4, and 5 have examined the first four areas of development in detail. This chapter will provide a brief overview of the research efforts related to FRBR with an additional focus on gaps in FRBR user research and other critical areas that require immediate attention.

FRBR RESEARCH OVERVIEW

Essentially, all FRBR-related efforts in the form of theoretical discussion, exploration, and development as well as practical evaluation and implementation could be considered FRBR research. As such, FRBR research covers a very diverse range of topics, including those that have been explored in the previous chapters. FRBR research has been the focus of a great deal of activity in recent years. According to version 13.2 of the *FRBR Bibliography* released in July 2008 (Functional Requirements for Bibliographic Records Review Group, 2008), there are 541 entries for FRBR-related publications, presentations, project Web sites, committee reports, project reports, blogs, and other materials, and more than 300 of the entries were created within the past five years. Only 40 percent of the entries are in the traditional, formal domain of publications such as journal articles, conference papers, books, book chapters, theses, and dissertations, while the remaining 60 percent of the entries are presentations, reports, working documents, and related Web sites. This ratio highlights the evolving and dynamic nature of this research area.

FRBR-related literature has appeared mainly in journals with cataloging and technical services themes as well as in books and conference proceedings. However, very few journals with broad coverage of the library and information science field have published articles on FRBR. For example, based on an analysis of coverage of the information organization-related literature in *Library Quarterly* during 1931–2004, there is a call for future journal coverage of FRBR along with other current issues in the area of information organization (Olson, 2006). In a comprehensive review of the cataloging and classification literature of 2003 and 2004, FRBR is identified as one of the major themes and is recognized as one of the major driving forces for changes in cataloging theory and practice (Miksa, 2007). In a more recent review of the cataloging and classification literature of 2005 and 2006, the importance of FRBR to the library community is also distinguished, and FRBR continues to generate a strong interest among librarians and researchers (El-Sherbini, 2008). FRBR-related literature shows a shift from being descriptive in nature to involving applications of the model in various environments, including online catalogs and electronic resources.

In the area of the FRBR model and model-related background and theory, which make up a major body of the FRBR literature, the topics under examination include providing the background of the model, interpreting and understanding the model, reviewing and evaluating the model, and associating the model with other models. As FRBR has undergone various applications and implementations, there have been discussions of FRBR model modifications meant to adapt the model in practice (Albertsen and van Nuys, 2005; Jones, 2005; Ayres, Fitch, and Kilner, 2003; O'Neill, 2002). In addition, ongoing developmental efforts have been made to extend the FRBR model to include authority data under the model of Functional Requirements for Authority Data (FRAD) and FRBR Group 3 entities under the model of Functional Requirements for Subject Authority Records (FRSAR)[1] to provide a more complete view of the bibliographic universe (Riva,

2007). Chapter 2 of this book provides an overview and discussion related to the FRBR model.

In the area of FRBR and related standards, FRBR has been influencing the development of future cataloging rules and new standards for library communities. Notably, the Joint Steering Committee for Development of RDA (JSC), charged with developing RDA (Resource Description and Access), plans to align "the structure, concepts and terminology of the instructions more directly with the Functional Requirements for Bibliographic Records (FRBR) and Functional Requirements for Authority Data (FRAD) models" (Joint Steering Committee for Revision of Anglo-American Cataloguing Rules, 2007: 2) and to "revise the instructions to facilitate collocation at the FRBR work and expression levels" (Joint Steering Committee for Revision of Anglo-American Cataloguing Rules, 2007: 3). The impact of FRBR on other related standards such as International Standard Bibliographic Description (ISBD), International Standard Serial Number (ISSN), Dublin Core, and MARC have also been examined and discussed (Riva, 2004, 2007; Network Development and MARC Standards Office, 2006; Antelman, 2004; Le Boeuf, 2001, 2002). Furthermore, the potential of FRBR to serve as a basis for creating uniform, international cataloging rules has also been investigated (Miksa, 2007). Chapter 3 of this book provides an overview and discussion related to FRBR standards and addresses the impact of FRBR on cataloging standards and practices.

FRBR has been widely applied in various collections of resources, including general library collections and subsets of library collections such as fiction, serials, and moving image materials, as well as some special collections and specific disciplines such as national literature, classical texts, electronic resources, hand press materials, live performing arts, music collections, and oral tradition works. In terms of application settings, FRBR has been applied in libraries, archives, consortia, digital libraries, and museums. While the various FRBR applications have been perceived as beneficial to users and effective for retrieval, specific application issues have been raised and discussed in articles about individual cases and in review articles collectively (Salaba and

Zhang, 2007; Noerr et al., 1998). Chapter 4 of this book reviews and discusses these issues.

FRBR system development involves the implementation and related evaluation of FRBR-based systems, from full-scale working systems to small-scale prototypes or experimental test systems as well as software tools and algorithms that facilitate building a working system. Current FRBR implementation projects are largely exploratory in nature without established best practices. FRBR implementation related issues have been explored, identified, and addressed by various individual projects as well as by collective reflections and evaluations of current implementation efforts (O'Neill, 2007; Žumer, 2007; Yee, 2005; Žumer and Riesthuis, 2002). Chapter 5 of this book reviews and discusses these issues related to FRBR implementations.

GAPS IN FRBR USER RESEARCH

Previous research has expounded the importance of understanding users' needs when designing effective online catalogs (Yee, 1991). In light of the changing environment for users and uses of bibliographic data in the Internet age, the conceptions of information resources, user expectations, user information seeking behavior, and information access have evolved and undergone major changes (Fallgren, 2007; Sadeh, 2007). It is critically necessary to understand users in order to build an effective bibliographic system, particularly in the three areas of future use of bibliographic data: (1) discovery and delivery, (2) inventory management, and (3) cross-compatibility with related data. FRBR is considered a user-centered framework for providing richer discovery and delivery (Fallgren, 2007). A survey of current literature and products of various types found that only recently have some of the commonly used Internet search features, such as faceted browsing and FRBRized display, begun to be introduced into library interfaces (Sadeh, 2007, 2008).

FRBR user research has been the least addressed facet of FRBR research and development. Current implementations have focused mainly on system development and adaptation of existing cataloging standards and practices to support user tasks as defined in FRBR (Ayres, 2005; Mimno, Crane, and Jones, 2005; Ayres, Fitch, and Kilner, 2003; O'Neill, 2002). Based on a review of FRBR implementation projects and a survey of the project leaders conducted by the authors of this book in Spring 2007, very few FRBR projects had actually conducted or reported user studies on their developed FRBR systems, although several had plans for such user testing. In addition, there had been no evaluative comparisons of existing FRBR prototype systems. To a great extent, the current FRBR application and implementation efforts have reflected the views of the designers and researchers with user considerations rather than the user views and validation directly. Additionally, there has been a gap in research pertaining to public library users. It is important that user studies of future online catalogs include this user group.

The recently released report by the Library of Congress Working Group on the Future of Bibliographic Control calls for more FRBR-related user testing and evaluation before further development of RDA (Working Group on the Future of Bibliographic Control, 2008). Indeed, as the FRBR model is widely embraced by library communities, future cataloging standards, library practice, and system development are expected to undergo major changes. Such changes should be informed by a thorough understanding of the FRBR model and its implications as well as by solid user evaluations of pilot FRBR system implementations, both of which are suspiciously underrepresented in the research.

Recently, some researchers have started conducting FRBR research that directly engages users in an attempt to fill the research gaps. As part of a three-year ongoing IMLS (Institute of Museum and Library Services) funded project on the research and development of FRBR-based retrieval systems to support user tasks and facilitate effective information seeking, Zhang and Salaba (2008) conducted a user study of current FRBR prototype systems, including OCLC FictionFinder (http://fictionfinder.oclc.org), WorldCat.org (www.worldcat.org), and the Libraries Australia's FRBR prototype demonstration system (http://ll01.nla.gov.au).

These three FRBR prototypes were evaluated and compared by 75 users from both public and academic library settings. This study showed there were noted differences in success by individual users in using the three systems when performing various FRBR tasks:

- "Find a work" tended to enjoy the highest success rate among all tasks across systems.
- "Find a set of works" and "find a similar work" tended to be completed successfully.
- "Find a manifestation" appeared to be difficult, particularly in FictionFinder.
- "Find an expression" appeared to be challenging, particularly in WorldCat.org.
- "Obtain/acquire" tended to have the lowest success rate.

When compared with users' local library catalog systems, the FRBR prototype systems appeared to be comparably supportive as measured by the success rate for the users' self-chosen tasks. In the study, users offered specific comments about the various system functions and features they found helpful or desirable when using the individual systems. The top ranked system functions and features that users liked include the following areas:

- Interface (user friendly, easy to use, and appealing)
- Links to related items in description (collocation by author, subject, and similarity)
- Refining options
- Additional information (ratings, reviews, price, audience summaries, format icons, etc.)
- Sorting options (by date, format, language, etc.)
- Availability/holding information

In addition, the users made detailed recommendations on the ways in which the FRBR prototype systems could be improved to facilitate information seeking. The most commonly mentioned areas for improvement include the following:

▶ Add more links to related works (collocation via "more like this," hyperlinked subjects, hyperlinked authors, series links, linked keywords, linked cited works, linking other formats from a desired work).

▶ Group and display information in results page (group into categories; arrange by language, date, author in alphabetical order; title in alphabetical order if an author search; multiple criteria).

▶ Add sorting options (by multiple criteria, age groups, date, language, relevance, etc.).

▶ Improve interface display (less clutter, large font, color to differentiate sorting and refining options, aesthetically pleasing, column display, bold letters for library information, highlighted searched terms in results page, highlighted resource summaries).

▶ Use clear labeling and terminology to avoid confusion.

▶ Allow advanced search options on the initial page.

In another recent study, Carlyle and Becker (2008) pretested a survey instrument to be used to examine the phenomenon of the known-item search by users of online catalogs. The purpose of the research was to evaluate the FRBR model as it pertains to describing entities that may help library users effectively search online catalogs. The study included 51 users, selected from both public and academic library users, who were looking for a specific book (known-item). The users were asked to respond to the survey instrument, which included various options for locating a substitute item related to the book they were looking for. Although still in an early stage, the study yielded findings that challenge some of the common assumptions about how users conduct known-item searches involving particular editions or publishers. The study reported that for known-item search, only 13 percent of the users indicated that they looked for a specific edition or book that had a particular publisher, 69 percent did not rely on edition or publisher for such searches, and 18 percent did not have a preference. When it comes to substitutability, the study found that the differences in manifestation (e.g., Web site versus physical print versions, paperback versus hardcover, regular print versus large print, etc.) were as important as those in expressions (e.g., unabridged versus abridged, languages). The findings of this study may help suggest ways in which different FRBR entities, such as manifestations and expressions, could be more effectively differentiated and how collocation of related works could be better supported in FRBR-based online catalogs.

Sadeh (2007, 2008) reported a usability study of the Primo discovery and delivery system from Ex Libris, which has a user interface that was designed based on "new-generation" user experiences obtained by surveying users' needs, preferences, behavior patterns, and evaluations of previous versions of the interface. The Primo groupings are based on FRBR with enhancements based on the feedback from both librarians and development partners. The system allows groupings of similar items by multiple editions or multiple translations of a book. Also, the system allows users to choose between a grouped display and an itemized display of all similar items in the search results. The usability study included eight users, including faculty, graduate students, and undergraduate students from various disciplines in both of the two sets of testing with the system's alpha and beta version respectively. User interactions with the system were captured using a think-aloud protocol, unobtrusive observation, screen captures, eye-tracking, and post-search interviews and evaluations. All the participants completed assigned tasks within an hour with minimal help and without any prior knowledge of the system. The participants evaluated the interface very positively, finding it to be friendly, easy to learn, and easier to use compared to other systems. They positively reviewed the faceted browsing as a useful way to narrow down the results list. Other features also received positive reviews, including the "Get it" service, the tagging capabilities, and the option to view only currently available items.

The above FRBR user research helps demarcate options for FRBR implementation and validates the development of more effective FRBR systems in the future. User studies of existing systems will also reveal current FRBR implementation issues and suggest possible solutions from users' perspectives. Future user research may further explore the nature of user needs and tasks, which will serve as the foundation for both the insightful application and the effective implementation of FRBR systems.

CRITICAL ISSUES AND CHALLENGES IN FRBR RESEARCH

The FRBR Delphi panel (see Chapter 1) raised five critical issues related to FRBR research as listed in the order of their importance:

▶ Issue 1: User studies on FRBR-based systems to ensure that implementations benefit end users

▶ Issue 2: User research on FRBR-based displays

▶ Issue 3: Examination of end user tasks with empirical research

▶ Issue 4: Automatic processing of databases or full-text electronic resources to facilitate FRBR implementation

▶ Issue 5: Development of semiotic frameworks and research to ensure effective communication between users and FRBR systems

Notably, four of the five issues are related to user research. Topping the list is the need to conduct user studies to ensure that FRBR-based implementations benefit end users. Although still puzzled by what a FRBRized system should offer end users and how to best present FRBR to the end users in terms of search dialogues and presentation of entities and relationships, the panel considered user studies as the top priority in FRBR research at the moment. Particularly, user research is important for justifying system development, figuring out the most appropriate methods to serve users, and better introducing FRBR from the users' perspective.

User research in FRBR-based displays is another critical issue that must be addressed in FRBR research. Some panel members are concerned that system developers currently do not see collocation as an essential feature for discovery. Hopefully, more user research on FRBR-based collocation displays will address this concern and allow users to take full advantage of this important discovery feature. An area in particular need of additional focused studies centers on user understanding of the display of complex works, which may help evaluate whether FRBR-based displays demonstrably improve user understanding. The panel also warned that user research on FRBR-based systems is not equal to testing FRBR-based displays, because the FRBR model could be most effective when it is working "behind the scenes."

The assumption behind the FRBR model is that it will better support user tasks. However, there has been a lack of empirical studies that validate this assumption or verify whether the user tasks as defined in the FRBR model indeed reflect user information seeking. Because user tasks will essentially decide the mandatory data elements and relationships in the bibliographic description as well as functions and interfaces for retrieval systems, it is important to verify the FRBR user tasks in the first place. Some suggested questions by the panel for future research in this area include the following:

▶ How many users come to the catalog looking for a particular manifestation but benefit from seeing other manifestations, expressions, and related works that they did not know existed?

▶ How many users come to the catalog looking for a particular work, not a particular manifestation?

▶ How many users come to the catalog looking for works that exist in a single manifestation? How many look for works that exist in multiple manifestations?

In addition, the panel suggested that user tasks should be evaluated and examined with consideration for specific communities where the tasks are performed and in light of the Internet environment in general and Web 2.0 in particular. Another research topic to explore in this area is the relevance of research of bibliographic data, which has been mostly absent compared to topic and system related relevance research.

Another critical issue in FRBR research is the facilitation of effective FRBR implementation, particularly in the area of automatic processing of databases or full-text electronic resources. This line of research is critical since current records and databases are not readily FRBR-compliant for accurate transformation, yet it is not realistic or feasible to recatalog existing materials. The panel suggested that better automated discovery and processing is the key to solving this problem. For example, in a large-scale FRBR-based catalog, this may involve finding multiple versions of the same work and organizing them into a hierarchical tree structure based on the Group 1 entities while linking them to other groups of entities. Although automatic linking of records and documents is one of the most promising areas for future FRBR research in an increasingly digital environment, challenges are also recognized, including insufficient information in current catalog records to perform this task accurately and incorrect linking that leads to compromised results.

Although not rated as important as other issues for future FRBR research, semiotic frameworks and approaches have been suggested as a possibility for communication studies focusing on the interpretation of meaning conveyed by cultural signs, which may help effective communication between users and FRBR systems and may facilitate dissemination of meanings from the enormous amount of information.

SUMMARY

FRBR research covers a very diverse range of topics and has been very active in recent years. FRBR is still relatively new; as such, it is rapidly evolving and full of opportunities and challenges. There are many emerging issues and unexplored areas at this early stage of development (O'Neill, 2007). Notably, while it has been discussed extensively by the library community that the FRBR model offers more opportunities for creating retrieval systems that support user information seeking than traditional retrieval systems, the literature shows a lack of research incorporating empirical user studies. Also, while all FRBR-related efforts could be considered FRBR research, the core research areas need to be identified. As library communities embrace the changes that the results of

FRBR research have encouraged, a clear direction for future FRBR development and research is vital for ongoing changes to future cataloging standards and practices, and, consequently, for the development of systems that better support user information seeking.

NOTE

1. As mentioned in Chapter 2 of this book, this model is called Functional Requirements for Subject Authority Data (FRSAD).

REFERENCES

Albertsen, Ketil, and Carol van Nuys. 2005. "Paradigma: FRBR and Digital Documents." *Cataloging & Classification Quarterly* 39, no. 3/4: 125–149.

Antelman, Kristin. 2004. "Identifying the Serial Work as a Bibliographic Entity." *Library Resources & Technical Services* 48, no. 4: 238–255.

Ayres, Marie-Louise. 2005. "Case Studies in Implementing Functional Requirements for Bibliographic Records [FRBR]: AustLit and MusicAustralia." *The Australian Library Journal* 54, no. 1: 43–54.

Ayres, Marie-Louise, Kent Fitch, and Kerry Kilner. 2003. "Report on the Successful AustLit: Australian Literature Gateway Implementation of the FRBR and INDECS Event Models, and Implications for Other FRBR Implementations." *International Cataloguing and Bibliographic Control: Quarterly Bulletin of the IFLA UBCIM Programme* 32, no. 1: 8–13.

Carlyle, Allyson, and Samantha R. Becker. 2008. "FRBR and the 'Known-Item' Search." In *Proceedings of the American Society for Information Science and Technology* (October 24–29), Columbus, OH: American Society for Information Science and Technology.

El-Sherbini, Magda A. 2008. "Cataloging and Classification: Review of the Literature 2005–2006." *Library Resources & Technical Services* 52, no. 3: 148–163.

Fallgren, Nancy J. 2007. *User and Uses of Bibliographic Data: Background Paper for the Working Group on the Future of Bibliographic Control.* Available: www.loc.gov/bibliographic-future/meetings/docs/Users andUsesBackgroundPaper.pdf (accessed July 30, 2009).

Functional Requirements for Bibliographic Records Review Group. 2008. "FRBR Bibliography." Available: www.ifla.org/en/node/881 (accessed July 30, 2009).

Joint Steering Committee for Revision of Anglo-American Cataloging Rules. 2007. "Strategic Plan for RDA 2005–2009." November 1. Available: www.rda-jsc.org/docs/5strategic1rev2.pdf (accessed July 30, 2009).

Jones, Ed. 2005. "The FRBR Model as Applied to Continuing Resources." *Library Resources & Technical Services* 49, no. 4: 227–242.

Le Boeuf, Patrick. 2001. "FRBR and Further." *Cataloging & Classification Quarterly* 32, no. 4: 15–52.

Le Boeuf, Patrick. 2002. "The Impact of the FRBR Model on the Future Revisions of the ISBDs: A Challenge for the IFLA Section on Cataloguing." *International Cataloguing and Bibliographic Control: Quarterly Bulletin of the IFLA UBCIM Programme* 31, no. 1: 3–6.

Miksa, Shawne D. 2007. "The Challenges of Change—A Review of Cataloging and Classification Literature, 2003–2004." *Library Resources & Technical Services* 51, no. 1: 51–68.

Mimno, David, Gregory Crane, and Allison Jones. 2005. "Hierarchical Catalog Records: Implementing a FRBR Catalog." *D-Lib Magazine* 11, no. 10. Available: www.dlib.org/dlib/october05/crane/10crane.html (accessed July 30, 2009).

Network Development and MARC Standards Office, Library of Congress. 2006. "Functional Analysis of the MARC 21 Bibliographic and Holdings Formats." Available: www.loc.gov/marc/marc-functional-analysis/functional-analysis.html (accessed July 30, 2009).

Noerr, Peter, Paula Goossens, Dan Matei, Petra Otten, Susanna Peruginelli, and Maria Witt. 1998. "User Benefits from a New Bibliographic Model: Follow-up of the IFLA Functional Requirements Study." *International Cataloguing and Bibliographic Control: Quarterly Bulletin of the IFLA UBCIM Programme* 28, no. 3: 80–81. Available: http://archive.ifla.org/IV/ifla64/084-126e.htm (accessed July 30, 2009).

Olson, Hope A. 2006. "Codes, Costs, and Critiques: The Organization of Information in Library Quarterly, 1931–2004." *Library Quarterly* 76, no. 1: 19–35.

O'Neill, Edward T. 2002. "FRBR: Functional Requirements for Bibliographic Records: Application of the Entity–Relationship Model to Humphry Clinker." *Library Resources & Technical Services* 46, no. 4: 150–159.

O'Neill, Edward T. 2007. "The Impact of Research on the Development of FRBR." In *Understanding FRBR: What It Is and How It Will Affect Our Retrieval Tools* (pp. 59–72), edited by Arlene G. Taylor. Westport, CT: Libraries Unlimited.

Riva, Pat. 2004. "Mapping MARC 21 Linking Entry Fields to FRBR and Tillett's Taxonomy of Bibliographic Relationships." *Library Resources & Technical Services* 48, no. 2: 130–143.

Riva, Pat. 2007. "Introducing the Functional Requirements for Bibliographic Records and Related IFLA Developments." *Bulletin of the American Society for Information Science and Technology* 33, no. 6: 7–11.

Sadeh, Tamar. 2007. "Time for a Change: New Approaches for a New Generation of Library Users." *New Library World* 108, no. 7/8: 307–316.

Sadeh, Tamar. 2008. "User Experience in the Library: A Case Study." *New Library World* 109, no. 1/2: 7–24.

Salaba, Athena, and Yin Zhang. 2007. "From a Conceptual Model to Application and System Development." *Bulletin of the American Society for Information Science and Technology* 33, no. 6: 17–23. Available: www.asis.org/Bulletin/Aug-07/Salaba_Zhang.pdf (accessed July 30, 2009).

Working Group on the Future of Bibliographic Control. 2008. "On the Record: Report of the Library of Congress Working Group on the Future of Bibliographic Control." Available: www.loc.gov/biblio graphic-future/news/lcwg-ontherecord-jan08-final.pdf (accessed July 30, 2009).

Yee, Martha M. 1991. "System Design and Cataloging Meet the User— User Interfaces to Online Public Access Catalogs." *Journal of the American Society for Information Science* 42, no. 2: 78–98.

Yee, Martha M. 2005. "FRBRization: A Method for Turning Online Public Finding Lists into Online Public Catalogs." *Information Technology and Libraries* 24, no. 2: 77–95.

Zhang, Yin, and Athena Salaba. 2008. "User Research and Testing of FRBR-Based Online Library Catalogs." Anaheim: Library Research Round Table (LRRT) Forums at 2008 ALA Annual Conference (June 26–July 2, 2008). Available: http://frbr.slis.kent.edu/presenta tions/FRBR-ALA-2008.pdf (accessed July 30, 2009).

Žumer, Maja. 2007. "FRBR: The End of the Road or a New Beginning." *Bulletin of the American Society for Information Science and Technology* 33, no. 6: 27–29. Available: www.asis.org/Bulletin/Aug-07/Zumer.pdf (accessed July 30, 2009).

Žumer, Maja, and Gerhard J. A. Riesthuis. 2002. "Consequences of Implementing FRBR: Are We Ready to Open Pandora's Box?" *Knowledge Organization* 29, no. 2: 78–86.

►7

CONCLUSIONS AND FUTURE DIRECTIONS FOR FRBR

F RBR (Functional Requirements for Bibliographic Records) was introduced in 1998 to address the challenges facing the library community in light of the changes in the cataloging environment driven by technological advances, economic pressures, and the increasing user focus of library services. Over the past decade, we have seen lively discussion, creative exploration, practical development, and active research around FRBR in an effort to respond to the challenges and seek the opportunities that FRBR may offer.

The objectives of this book have been to provide an overview of the current status of FRBR development, to identify the key FRBR issues that need to be addressed, and to point to future directions of FRBR development. The individual chapters of this book presented a detailed account of the current status, key issues, and future directions of each of the five FRBR developmental fronts: the FRBR model, FRBR and current cataloging standards and practice, FRBR application, FRBR implementation, and FRBR research. This concluding chapter will present a unified overview of the development, issues, and future directions.

FRBR DEVELOPMENT

FRBR-related advances have been made and are emerging on all five developmental fronts as summarized in the following sections.

The FRBR Model

The review and discussion of the FRBR model and its potential in addressing the challenges facing the library community have been major topics of FRBR research. FRBR offers a new perspective of the bibliographic universe and has been recognized for its potential to help develop better information systems for users, improve cataloging efforts, and better manage resources in a digital environment. However, it is important to note that FRBR is still evolving. For example, an amendment to FRBR is underway to address problems encountered in modeling "aggregate" works. Currently, the FRBR model is being extended and connected to two other models, FRAD (Functional Requirements for Authority Data) and FRSAD (Functional Requirements for Subject Authority Data).[1] Jointly, these three models will provide a view of the bibliographic universe that is significantly more comprehensive and that includes all entities in the three FRBR groups as well as their relationships (Riva, 2007). In addition, FRBR has been actively reviewed for possible refinements and applications in communities beyond traditional library settings. Because of the abstract and evolving nature of the FRBR model, interpreting and understanding it still pose a challenge and require continuing effort (Maxwell, 2008; Riva, 2007; Carlyle, 2006).

FRBR and Related Cataloging Standards and Practice

Due to the great potential benefits that FRBR may offer, FRBR has been embraced by library communities and continues to shape the direction of future cataloging principles, rules, and related standards. Notably, FRBR has been reflected in the revisions and development of the International Cataloguing Principles, ISBD (International Standard Bibliographic Description), RDA (Resource Description and Access), RDA DC (Dublin Core) Application Profile, and MARC. Because FRBR represents a bibliographic universe that can potentially include any information accessible to users, the potential of FRBR to serve as a basis for creating uniform, international cataloging rules has also been investigated (Miksa, 2007; Tillett, 2005). As a result of such imminent changes, current cataloging practice must be adjusted accordingly, although the specifics and extent of the resulting changes still remain to be seen.

FRBR Application

In terms of application settings, FRBR has been applied in traditional libraries, archives, consortia, digital libraries, institutional repositories, Web portals, and museums. FRBR has been applied in a variety of collections of resources, including general library collections and subsets of library collections such as fiction, serials and other continuing resources, and moving image materials. FRBR application has also been extended to various disciplines and some special collections such as works of art, national literature, classical texts, music collections, hand-press materials, oral tradition works, and the live performing arts. Although FRBR is still being tested with various collections and there are many practical issues that need to be resolved, it is believed that the collections that will benefit most from FRBR are those containing works with multiple expressions and manifestations.

FRBR Implementation

Various FRBR implementation efforts are underway to create retrieval systems that are more effective and better support user tasks. These efforts vary in scope and form, including theoretical discussion, user evaluation, and practical recommendation of implementation approaches; actual creation of prototypes or service systems; and development of full system software applications, software algorithms, tools, and utilities to facilitate the FRBR implementation process. Currently, due to a lack of implementation guidelines and best practices, FRBR implementations are largely exploratory in nature. While FRBR implementations related to online catalogs share a common goal of facilitating user tasks, various implementations, however, may differ in implementation approaches, the model focus for implementation, collection, record creation or conversion approach, system user interface and display, and system architecture and other system details. It is noted that current implementation efforts fall short of conducting user testing.

FRBR Research

FRBR research has been very active in recent years, covering a very diverse range of topics. While all FRBR-related efforts could be considered FRBR research, FRBR user research that incorporates empirical user studies has been particularly lacking. Such research has started to emerge in the past two years with direct user involvement in testing the FRBR model with specific user tasks (Carlyle and Becker, 2008), evaluating FRBR implementations (Sadeh, 2007, 2008; Zhang and Salaba, 2008), and getting feedback regarding implementation improvements (Sadeh, 2007, 2008; Zhang and Salaba, 2008). Such FRBR user research will help not only validate and refine the FRBR model but also help delineate useful approaches for effective FRBR implementations from the users' perspectives.

KEY FRBR ISSUES

The key issues in various FRBR developmental fronts as identified by the FRBR experts in the Delphi study have been profiled in the relevant individual chapters of this book (see Chapters 2–6 for details). This section will focus on the most important issues across all FRBR areas.

Overall, eight issues received a mean importance rating of 8 or higher (out of a ten-point scale) with a strong group consensus among the FRBR experts, and thus emerged as the most critical issues across all FRBR areas. These issues are listed in Table 7-1 from highest to lowest rating.

The development of cataloging rules in line with FRBR stands out as the most critical issue among all the issues raised and rated. Closely related, there are also calls for rules and standards for FRBR-based record structures as well as record encoding standards and frameworks for FRBR implementations (ranked #2). In addition, FRBR-oriented authority work standards for FRBR implementations are also critical (ranked #6A). Collectively, these issues stress the vital need for developing standards and rules to guide FRBR implementations.

For FRBR implementations, developing tools and software to facilitate automated FRBRization processes (ranked #3), and

▶TABLE 7-1. Most Critical FRBR Issues Overall		
Overall rank	Issue	Mean rating
1	Need to develop cataloging rules in line with FRBR.	9.00
2	Need to address FRBR-based record structures, record encoding standards, and frameworks for FRBR implementations.	8.40
3	Need to develop and test tools/software that will facilitate the FRBRization processes.	8.25
4A	Need to explore, develop, and test various means of FRBR implementation.	8.06
4B	Need to conduct user studies on FRBR-based systems to ensure that implementations benefit end users.	8.06
6A	Need to develop FRBR-oriented authority work standards for FRBR implementations.	8.00
6B	Need to verify and validate the FRBR model against real data and in different communities to make sure the model is valid and applicable.	8.00
6C	Need to address the FRBRization of existing data from a variety of differing standards and practices.	8.00

exploring, developing, and testing various implementation approaches (ranked #4A) appear to be critical. Also, FRBRization of existing data needs to be addressed from a variety of differing standards and practices (ranked #6C).

Not surprisingly, user research emerged as one of the most critical issues for overall FRBR development. It is important to conduct user studies on FRBR-based systems to ensure that implementations benefit end users (ranked #4B). Such user research will also serve as the basis for developing related standards, rules, and library practice for better user services. Finally, for the FRBR model itself, verifying and validating the model using real data and in different communities should be addressed (ranked #6B). More details of the FRBR issues are reported in "What Is Next for FRBR? A Delphi Study" (Zhang and Salaba, 2009).

FUTURE DIRECTIONS FOR FRBR

Although there are still many pressing issues that need to be addressed, FRBR-related development has made great progress in the past decade on many developmental fronts and is still evolving rapidly. With new cataloging standards and rules being developed and implemented and with the advances of information technologies, it is expected that FRBR will help develop more effective information systems to support user information needs and information seeking in the Internet environment. Future directions may be summarized in the following areas.

User Perspective for Future FRBR Development

Although FRBR has a strong user focus, current FRBR development has largely reflected researchers' or developers' perspectives for the user, and there has essentially been little to no user research done in FRBR, particularly from users' perspectives (Zhang and Salaba, 2008; Carlyle, 2006). Through thorough user research, users' perspectives should be incorporated and reflected in all FRBR developmental fronts in the future. In particular:

▶ The FRBR model itself needs to be verified by user research, and further model development needs to be informed by such user perspectives. For example, are the users' tasks as defined by FRBR really an adequate reflection of real users' needs and of the way users look for information? Future user studies need to look into the nature of user needs and tasks. These studies will then serve as the foundation for development of related cataloging standards, rules, and practice as well as for effective FRBR applications and implementations.

▶ Cataloging standards and practices that are created based on FRBR should also be informed by adequate user studies. It is not surprising that the report by the Library of Congress Working Group on the Future of Bibliographic Control calls for more FRBR-related user testing and evaluation before further development of RDA (Working Group on the Future of Bibliographic Control, 2008). Such development is worth the effort only when the proposed changes to the cataloging standards and practices are truly beneficial to various users, including end users, catalogers, and other user groups.

▶ As FRBR is applied in various settings, collections, and disciplines, the user communities involved in each application may have user needs, tasks, and considerations that are specific to the setting, collection, and discipline. The interpretation of the FRBR model, such as Group 1 entities, and the subsequent application may also vary as a result of the differences in user considerations.

▶ Various FRBR implementation approaches and products should be designed based on and informed by user studies and should subsequently be tested and evaluated by users so that design and implementation guidelines that truly benefit users can be developed for future FRBR implementations.

▶ Finally, it is noted that current user research has been largely limited to end users. Other user groups, as defined by the FRBR model, such as library staff, publishers, distributors, retailers, and providers as well as users of information services outside the traditional library setting, have been left out in current FRBR user studies. Future user research should include various user groups.

FRBR for Information Discovery Beyond Catalogs

One of the future trends for library catalogs is to serve as a discovery tool in the Internet environment and to provide easy information discovery and effortless connections between users and the information resources they are seeking (Calhoun, 2006; Dempsey, 2006). FRBR has the potential to accommodate data on a wide range of materials, media, and formats beyond traditional library records, and it can foster easier integrations of resources and systems among libraries and beyond in the digital information environment (International Federation of Library Associations and Institutions Study Group, 1998). In light of the changing environment for users and uses of bibliographic data in the Internet age, where federated searching of integrated resources is a common practice, FRBR is considered a user-centered framework for providing users with richer discovery and delivery (Fallgren, 2007). Specifically, FRBR can contribute toward the future integration of "all resources in all of the world's repositories, including libraries, bookstores, music and film archives, publishing houses, etc.," supporting the searching of "all potential sources of information" (Tillett, 2005: 202). The recent development of the eXtensible Catalog (XC) software (see www.extensiblecatalog.org) is a very exciting move in this direction. XC allows libraries to harvest and integrate metadata from multiple sources and to provide end users an effective discovery tool with FRBR features, faceted browsing, and many other features that come with the Drupal Web-based content management system, including Web 2.0 features.

Open Source Approach

As reviewed in Chapter 5, many FRBR implementation projects have produced open source software that is freely available under various open source licenses. Such open source software supports a range of activities from creating a whole FRBR system to supporting certain aspects of a system such as the FRBRization of MARC records and the creation of user interfaces based on the FRBR model.

It is noted that open source developers are joining forces to incorporate FRBR. Notably, the two most popular open source integrated library systems, Koha and Evergreen, have developed FRBR functions. Specifically, Koha's FRBR module uses OCLC's xISBN and LibraryThing's ThingISBN to link records for various editions of works, while Evergreen supports grouping various editions and formats of the same title together. Also, the XC software is developed to work with Drupal, a popular open source Web-based content management system widely used in libraries. Such enhancement of existing open source software and integration of existing open source products will help build collaborations and communities of users and developers. Future FRBR implementations will benefit greatly from this open source development approach, which will make it much easier for individual libraries to implement FRBR.

Effective Processing of Legacy Data

Libraries have invested heavily in and contributed significantly to creating metadata. MARC records alone represent the cumulative efforts of over four decades. We need to deal with library legacy data to either create a FRBR-based online catalog or integrate library data with other sources in a heterogeneous system that supports FRBR. Given the large amount and record structure of such legacy data, developing software tools are essential for the effective processing, cleaning, normalizing, integrating, and sharing of data automatically and with the least amount of human intervention possible. Among the challenges and issues discussed in Chapter 5 regarding legacy data, it is essential to define the identifiers for various FRBR entities, on which there has not been a commonly established approach despite much discussion over the years (Carlyle, Ranger, and Sumlnerlin, 2008; Yee, 2005; Le Boeuf, 2001). This issue needs to be resolved before FRBRization of legacy data is achievable.

CONCLUDING REMARKS

Since FRBR was introduced in 1998, library and information communities have been actively engaging in the fascinating and productive endeavor of exploring FRBR. This book offers an overview of the current status of FRBR by summarizing and discussing the FRBR-related development and key issues on five fronts: the FRBR model, FRBR and current cataloging standards and practice, FRBR application, FRBR implementation, and FRBR research. The past decade has seen a shift of FRBR development from the initial purely theoretical discussion to practical implementations on all developmental fronts. The fruitful development effort has been making progress in turning this abstract conceptual model into concrete library standards, practices, and systems that aim to better support users' information seeking as well as library functions and services in today's information environment and in the future.

It is an exciting time for implementing FRBR in libraries as new FRBR-based cataloging standards and rules are being developed, systems and tools are being built, and best practices and implementation guidelines are emerging. For future FRBR development, it is essential to incorporate and reflect user perspectives for a truly successful FRBR implementation.

NOTE

1. As mentioned in Chapter 2 of this book, this model is called Functional Requirements for Subject Authority Data (FRSAD).

REFERENCES

Calhoun, Karen. 2006. "The Changing Nature of the Catalog and Its Integration with Other Discovery Tools." Available: www.loc.gov/catdir/calhoun-report-final.pdf (accessed July 30, 2009).

Carlyle, Allyson. 2006. "Understanding FRBR as a Conceptual Model: FRBR and the Bibliographic Universe." *Library Resources & Technical Services* 50, no. 4: 264–273.

Carlyle, Allyson, and Samantha R. Becker. 2008. "FRBR and the 'Known-Item' Search." In *Proceedings of the American Society for Information Science and Technology* (October 24–29). Columbus, OH: American Society for Information Science and Technology.

Carlyle, Allyson, Sara Ranger, and Joel Sumlnerlin. 2008. "Making the Pieces Fit: *Little Women*, Works, and the Pursuit of Quality." *Cataloging & Classification Quarterly* 46, no. 1: 35–63.

Dempsey, Lorcan. 2006. "The Library Catalogue in the New Discovery Environment: Some Thoughts." *Ariadne* 48. Available: www.ariadne.ac.uk/issue48/dempsey (accessed July 30, 2009).

Fallgren, Nancy J. 2007. "User and Uses of Bibliographic Data: Background Paper for the Working Group on the Future of Bibliographic Control." Available: www.loc.gov/bibliographic-future/meetings/docs/UsersandUsesBackgroundPaper.pdf (accessed July 30, 2009).

International Federation of Library Associations and Institutions Study Group on the Functional Requirements for Bibliographic Records. 1998. *Functional Requirements for Bibliographic Records: Final Report.* Munich, Germany: K. G. Saur. Available: www.ifla.org/en/publications/functional-requirements-for-bibliographic records (accessed July 30, 2009).

Le Boeuf, Patrick. 2001. "FRBR and Further." *Cataloging & Classification Quarterly* 32, no. 4: 15–52.

Maxwell, Robert L. 2008. *FRBR: A Guide for the Perplexed.* Chicago: American Library Association.

Miksa, Shawne D. 2007. "The Challenges of Change—A Review of Cataloging and Classification Literature, 2003–2004." *Library Resources & Technical Services* 51, no. 1: 51–68.

Riva, Pat. 2007. "Introducing the Functional Requirements for Bibliographic Records and Related IFLA Developments." *Bulletin of the American Society for Information Science and Technology* 33, no. 6: 7–11.

Sadeh, Tamar. 2007. "Time for a Change: New Approaches for a New Generation of Library Users." *New Library World* 108, no. 7/8: 307–316.

Sadeh, Tamar. 2008. "User Experience in the Library: A Case Study." *New Library World* 109, no. 1/2: 7–24.

Tillett, Barbara B. 2005. "FRBR and Cataloging for the Future." *Cataloging & Classification Quarterly* 39, no. 3/4: 197–205.

Working Group on the Future of Bibliographic Control. 2008. "On the Record: Report of the Library of Congress Working Group on the Future of Bibliographic Control." Available: www.loc.gov/bibliographic-future/news/lcwg-ontherecord-jan08-final.pdf (accessed July 30, 2009).

Yee, Martha M. 2005. "FRBRization: A Method for Turning Online Public Finding Lists into Online Public Catalogs." *Information Technology and Libraries* 24, no. 2: 77–95.

Zhang, Yin, and Athena Salaba. 2008. "User Research and Testing of FRBR-Based Online Library Catalogs." Anaheim: Library Research Round Table (LRRT) Forums at 2008 ALA Annual Conference (June 26–July 2, 2008). Available: http://frbr.slis.kent.edu/presentations/FRBR-ALA-2008.pdf (accessed July 30, 2009).

Zhang, Yin, and Athena Salaba. 2009. "What Is Next for FRBR? A Delphi Study." *The Library Quarterly* 79, no. 2: 233–255.

►Appendix A

ACRONYMS

Acronym	Full Name/Title
AACR	*Anglo-American Cataloguing Rules*
AACR2	*Anglo-American Cataloguing Rules*, Second Edition
ALCTS	Association for Library Collections and Technical Services
ANBD	Australian National Bibliographic Database
API	Application Programming Interface
AustLit	Australian Literature Resource
CC:DA	American Library Association's Committee on Cataloging: Description and Access
CCO	Cataloging Cultural Objects
CDWA	Categories for the Description of Works of Art
CIDOC	International Committee for Museum Documentation
CIDOC CRM	International Committee for Museum Documentation Conceptual Reference Model
CRM	Conceptual Reference Model
DACS	Department of Defense Information Analysis Center
DC	Dublin Core
DCAM	Dublin Core Abstract Model
DCMI	Dublin Core Metadata Initiative
DCMI/RDA Task Group	Dublin Core Metadata Initiative/Resource Description and Access Task Group
DLF	Digital Library Federation
DTD	Document Type Definition
EDItEUR	International Group For Electronic Commerce in the Book and Serials Sectors
FRAD	Functional Requirements for Authority Data

Acronym	Full Name/Title
FRANAR	Functional Requirements and Numbering of Authority Records
FRBR	Functional Requirements for Bibliographic Records
FRBR/CRM Harmonization Group	Functional Requirements for Bibliographic Records/ Conceptual Reference Model Harmonization Group
FRBRoo	Functional Requirements for Bibliographic Records–object-oriented
FRSAD	Functional Requirements for Subject Authority Data
FRSAR	Functional Requirements for Subject Authority Records
FRSAR WG	Functional Requirements for Subject Authority Records Working Group
FVWG	Format Variation Working Group
GMD	General Material Designators
GMD/SMD Working Group	General Material Designators/Standard Material Designation Working Group
ICADL	International Conference on Asian Digital Libraries
ICBC	International Cataloguing and Bibliographic Control
ICOM CIDOC	International Council of Museums International Committee for Documentation
ICOM CIDOC CRM	International Council of Museums International Committee for Documentation Conceptual Reference Model
IFLA	International Federation of Library Associations and Institutions
IFLA FRBR/CRM	IFLA Functional Requirements for Bibliographic Records/Conceptual Reference Model
IFLA FRBR Review Group	IFLA Functional Requirements for Bibliographic Records Review Group
IFLA WG on the Expression Entity	IFLA Working Group on the Expression Entity
IFLA WG on FRBR/ CRM Dialogue	IFLA Working Group on Functional Requirements for Bibliographic Records/Conceptual Reference Model Dialogue
IFPA	ISIS FRBR Prototype Application
III	Innovative Interfaces Inc.
ILS	Integrated Library System

Acronym	Full Name/Title
IME ICC	IFLA Meetings of Experts on an International Cataloguing Code
IMLS	Institute of Museum and Library Services
ISADN	International Standard Authority Data Number
ISBD	International Standard Bibliographic Description
ISSN	International Standard Serial Number
JSC	Joint Steering Committee for Revision of AACR (now Joint Steering Committee for Development of RDA)
JSC FVWG	Joint Steering Committee for Revision of AACR Format Variation Working Group
LDOW	Linked Data on the Web
LRRT	Library Research Round Table
MARBI	Machine-Readable Bibliographic Information
MARC	Machine-Readable Cataloging
MARC21	Machine-Readable Cataloging 21 (Formerly USMARC and CANMARC)
NACO	Name Authority Cooperative Program
NCSU	North Carolina State University
NDMSO	Network Development and MARC Standards Office
NSDL	National Science Digital Library
OAI PMH	Open Archives Initiative Protocol for Metadata Harvesting
OCLC	Online Computer Library Center
ONIX	Online Information Exchange
OPAC	Online Public Access Catalog
OTW	Oral Tradition Work
PDL	Perseus Digital Library
RDA	Resource Description and Access
RDA/DC Application Profile	Resource Description and Access/Dublin Core Application Profile
RDA/MARC WG	Resource Description and Access/Machine-Readable Cataloging Working Group

Acronym	Full Name/Title
RDA/ONIX	Resource Description and Access/Online Information Exchange
RDF	Resource Description Framework
RICA	Regole italiane di catalogazione per autori
SaaS	Software as a Service
UBCIM	Universal Bibliographic Control and International MARC Core Activity
UCLA	University of California–Los Angeles
UNIMARC	Universal Machine-Readable Cataloguing
URI	Uniform Resource Identifiers
VIAF	Virtual International Authority File
VTLS	Visionary Technology in Library Solutions
W3C	World Wide Web Consortium
WG	Working Group
XC	eXtensible Catalog
XML	eXtensible Markup Language
XML DTD	eXtensible Markup Language Document Type Definition
XSLT	eXtensible Stylesheet Language Transformations

FRBR IMPLEMENTATION EXAMPLES

ABC Harmony

Developer(s): Cornell Digital Library Research Group, USA; Distributed
  Systems Technology Centre, Australia; Institute for Learning and
  Research Technology UK
URL: www.ilrt.bris.ac.uk/discovery/harmony

ABC Harmony investigates the description of multimedia resources and the relationships between the components of these complex resources in a variety of digital environments, such as in archives, museums, or the Internet, through collaboration with metadata communities. An additional project goal is the development of a conceptual model to support interoperability across domain- or community-specific metadata vocabularies using W3C technologies. More information is also available at www.metadata.net/harmony/ABCV2.htm.

AustLit

Developer(s): National Library of Australia and twelve Australian
  Universities
URL: www.austlit.edu.au

AustLit has implemented the FRBR model for the description of literary and creative resources. It makes use of the FRBR entities work, expression (version in AustLit), and manifestation (publication in AustLit) to organize a collection of fictional literature by Australian authors or about Australian topics. The item entity, though not explicitly used in AustLit, is represented in the holdings of individual libraries. Additionally, AustLit has augmented the FRBR model with event modeling drawn from the INDECS and ABC Harmony models.

BIBSYS

Developer(s): Norwegian National Library, Norwegian University of Science
and Technology, Library of Norway
URL: www.bibsys.no

BIBSYS is an experimental system designed to research possible methods for applying the FRBR framework to existing MARC databases. This project resulted in a tool for interpreting and extracting FRBR elements from MARC records based on the FRBR model.

*d*Collection

Developer(s): Korean Education and Research Information Service (KERIS)
URL: www.dcollection.net/search/ko/main.do

*d*Collection is a collective digital repository for Korean universities. In a usability study of the repository, it was decided that FRBR's ability to cluster related works offered the best way to meaningfully group the large number of nationally sponsored project reports and their derivative works found in *d*Collection.

E-Matrix

Developer(s): North Carolina State University Libraries
URL: www.lib.ncsu.edu/e-matrix

E-Matrix is designed to manage serials and electronic resources. Based on the Digital Library Federation (DLF) Electronic Resource Management Initiative, this system makes use of FRBR terms such as *work* and *manifestation* as well as using the term *holding* in a way that is similar to the FRBR item entity. However, these terms are not directly linked to the FRBR model despite being used in a parallel fashion.

eXtensible Catalog (XC)

Developer(s): University of Rochester Libraries
URL: www.extensiblecatalog.org

The eXtensible Catalog is an ongoing project to develop open source tools for building a system that can access both traditional and digital library holdings. Its features will include the FRBRization of metadata and crosswalking between various metadata schemas as well as allowance for future adoption of Resource Description and Access (RDA). This project focuses on Group 1 FRBR entities instead of a full FRBR implementation.

FictionFinder

Developer(s): Online Computer Library Center (OCLC)

URL: http://fictionfinder.oclc.org

FictionFinder is an experimental system based on the subset of works of fiction from the WorldCat database. The OCLC Work-Set Algorithm groups materials together at the work level. In addition to traditional searches for title, author, and subject, FictionFinder supports searches for fictitious characters, literary awards, and book summaries. Search results are arranged by work and within each work by a combination of the expression and manifestation entities. Search results can be refined by language or format and can also be sorted according to various attributes.

FRBR Display Tool

Developer(s): Network Development and MARC Standards Office, Library of Congress

URL: www.loc.gov/marc/marc-functional-analysis/tool.html

The FRBR Display Tool is a free application that creates FRBR displays based on data extracted from MARC records. This tool allows libraries to experiment with FRBR without changing catalog records but still provides library users with better collocating and sorting of retrieved records by grouping them into the work, expression, and manifestation FRBR entities.

FRBR Floater

Developer(s): Monte Sano Associates

URL: www.montesanoassociates.com/apps-msafrbr.htm

FRBR Floater is a subscription service that enables users to view, via a pop-up OPAC window, various editions and formats of items in a particular library given any title searched if the search results in more than one edition or format. It will help library users browse a structured list and identify and select materials.

IFPA (ISIS FRBR Prototype Application)

Developer(s): Roberto Sturman, University of Trieste

URL: http://pclib3.ts.infn.it/frbr/wwwisis/FRB2.01/FORM.HTM

IFPA (ISIS FRBR Prototype Application) is an experimental FRBR tool developed to manage data and relationships according to the FRBR model, and it serves as an application for the UNESCO ISIS retrieval software. IFPA 2, the most recent version of the tool, can manage FRBR entities, their attributes, and entity relationships. An online demonstration is available at the project Web site.

INDECS

Developer(s): Indecs Framework Ltd
URL: www.doi.org/topics/indecs/indecs_framework_2000.pdf (project
    report)

INDECS was created to make interoperability between disparate databases containing information describing intellectual property possible. Though not a description schema in and of itself, the model is meant to interact with schema like FRBR, CIDOC from the museum community, and ONIX from the book industry. More information is available at http://cordis.europa.eu/econtent/mmrcs/indecs.htm#what.

Innovative Interfaces

Developer(s): Innovative Interfaces, Inc. (III)
URL: www.iii.com

Innovative Interfaces has investigated the potential integration of FRBR into their line of products, specifically the Millennium ILS, to enable systems to return structured search results of works available in many different versions, formats, and languages. However, further development and product release is on hold pending the release of the RDA standard.

Kent State University FRBR Project

Developer(s): Kent State University School of Library and Information
    Science
URL: http://frbr.slis.kent.edu

The Kent State University FRBR Project is intended to survey, examine, and compare FRBR-related research in order to develop an open source FRBR-based catalog. The collection used by the system contains bibliographic and authority records taken from the Library of Congress records in OCLC WorldCat.

LibDB

Developer(s): Morbus

URL: http://sourceforge.net/projects/libdb

LibDB is open source software for library and asset management inspired by FRBR, RDF triples, and end-usability. It supports cataloging of all types of resources, such as movies, books, comics, and serials.

LibraryLabs of Libraries Australia

Developer(s): National Library of Australia, National Australian Bibliographic Database

URL: http://ll01.nla.gov.au

This project is a Libraries Australia FRBR prototype, an experimental system that does not yet support regular library operations. It is described by its developers as "FRBR-like." Based on the Australian National Bibliographic Database, users can access this system via a hyperlink on the search result display page. Items are first grouped by type (book, musical score, film, etc.), then by language, and finally by the year of publication and publisher. In addition to the four FRBR entities, Libraries Australia also makes use of a superwork entity.

National Palace Museum's FRBR for Metadata Project

Developer(s): The National Palace Museum, Taipei

URL: www.npm.gov.tw/en/home.htm (museum site)

The National Palace Museum houses a large collection of Chinese artifacts and has conducted a study to determine the feasibility of supplementing its CDWA metadata with the FRBR model. The test collection consisted of Chinese paintings and calligraphy, and it was found that the FRBR model's emphasis on the work and expression entities mirrored the museum's own emphasis, showing FRBR to be a useful way to understand relationships in nontraditional collections. Information about the project is not available at the museum's site but is detailed in the following paper:

Chen, Yaning, and Shu-jiun Chen. 2004. "A Metadata Practice of the IFLA FRBR Model: A Case Study for the National Palace Museum in Taipei." *Journal of Documentation* 60, no. 2: 128–143.

OCLC Work-Set Algorithm

Developer(s): Online Computer Library Center (OCLC)

URL: www.oclc.org/research/software/frbr/default.htm

The OCLC FRBR Work-Set Algorithm was developed to examine the issues associated with the automatic FRBRization process and serve as a basis for implementing FRBR prototype systems on a large scale. The algorithm uses both authority records and bibliographic records to cluster catalog records at the work level.

OpenFRBR

Developer(s): William Denton

URL: www.openfrbr.org

OpenFRBR is an open source software tool for FRBR implementation. The most recent version can perform a partial implementation, though expansion to include more relationships is expected. Currently, the project site offers a demonstration of how the software may work.

Paradigma

Developer(s): National Library of Norway

URL: No longer available

The Paradigma project is a collection of digital documents acquired as part of the Norwegian Legal Deposit Act. Paradigma has adopted the FRBR framework as the basis for organizing Internet documents as a part of this project. Due to the changing nature of Internet documents, it was necessary to modify some FRBR elements, particularly the manifestation and item entities, so that they would be able to reflect the temporal aspects of archived Internet documents. Information about this project is available in the following article:

Albertsen, Ketil, and Carol van Nuys. 2005. "Paradigma: FRBR and Digital Documents." *Cataloging & Classification Quarterly* 39, no. 3/4: 125–149.

Perseus Digital Library

Developer(s): Tufts University

URL: www.perseus.tufts.edu/hopper

The Perseus Digital Library is a hierarchical catalog of classical texts that focuses on the work, expression, and manifestation entities. Because the collection's manifestation records often contain compilations of various separate works, the catalog has emphasized part-whole linkages between the work, expression, and manifestation entities.

RedLightGreen
Developer(s): Research Libraries Group (now part of OCLC)
URL: No longer available
One of the first FRBR-based systems, RedLightGreen has been largely replaced by WorldCat.org. Though this catalog made use of the work, expression, manifestation, and item framework of FRBR, it was not an entirely FRBRized system. Specifically, Red-LightGreen used both work and expression to correspond to the "title clusters," manifestation to correspond to specific editions, and items to correspond to items.

Tool for Converting Bibliographic Records
Developer(s): Norwegian National Library, Norwegian University of Science
    and Technology, Library of Norway
URL: www.ercim.org/publication/Ercim_News/enw66/aalberg.html
Developed as part of the BIBSYS project, this tool converts information held in MARC records into a format that reflects the FRBR model. This tool supports the full conversion of data in MARC records to reflect FRBR entities, attributes, and relationships.

UCLA Film and Television Archive OPAC
Developer(s): UCLA Film and Television Archive
URL: www.cinema.ucla.edu
The UCLA Film and Television Archive OPAC is a fully operational FRBR system with the goal of making available and preserving films of all varieties. This catalog, which uses the Voyager Integrated Library System, treats authority records as work records, bibliographic records as expression records, and holdings records as manifestation records.

Variations
Developer(s): Indiana University
URL: http://variations2.indiana.edu
Variations is a working system designed around an entity-relationship model, much like FRBR. Based on a collection of music represented

in audio and video files, scores, and computerized scores, Variations2 is the most current version in use, though work on Variations3 began in 2005.

Virtua Integrated Library System
Developer(s): VTLS (Visionary Technology in Library Solutions)
URL: www.vtls.com/products/virtua
The Virtua Integrated Library System software allows for the integration of FRBR-based records with traditional bibliographic records. Depending on the record accessed, the system can display a hierarchical FRBR view of work, expression, manifestation, and item. VLTS also offers a Software as a Service (SaaS) option for the FRBR display that can be linked from a library's catalog to a VTLS server.

VisualCat
Developer(s): Portia
URL: www.portia.dk/websites/productgallery.htm
VisualCat is a cataloging software system developed and distributed by Portia. It has been developed as an integrated solution for copy cataloging and bibliographic metadata management within a single framework based on RDF and FRBR. It can be used to develop a cataloging client or integrated library system that is capable of serving an accurate, user-friendly catalog. However, no new information about the product has been available at its main Web site since 2005.

WorldCat.org
Developer(s): Online Computer Library Center (OCLC)
URL: http://worldcat.org
WorldCat.org is a fully operational, worldwide, multilingual catalog that includes records for books, music, videos, digital audiobooks, article citations, documents and photos of historical note, and digital versions of rare items. The catalog is based on the OCLC WorldCat but provides open access. It uses the OCLC Work-Set Algorithm to group records by work. Additionally, it makes use of a faceted search display.

Only acronyms are used as index entries; expansions are located in Appendix A. Locators followed by "f" indicate figures; locators followed by "t" indicate tables. Italicized locators indicate terms included in Appendix A or Appendix B.

A

AACR, 29, 36–38, 46, 98, *135*
ABC Harmony, 62, *139*
Acquire (user task). *See* User tasks
Aggregates, 21, 23, 24, 57, 64, 66–67, 124
ALCTS, *135*
Algorithms. *See* Implementation; System design
ANBD, 68, *135, 143*
API, 86, *135*
Application
  benefits (*see* Benefits of FRBR)
  challenges, 70
  collections (*see individual collection types*, e.g., Aggregates)
  FRBR Delphi study, 70
  settings (*see individual setting types*, e.g., Consortia)
Archives, 7, 28, 34, 75, 93, 104, 111, 125, 130, *139*. *See also* Internet archives; UCLA Film and Television Archive
Attributes, 14, 21–22, 29–30, 33, 66
  definition, 2
  and implementation projects, 81, 88, 89, 90, 102 (*see also individual implementation project names*)
  mapping to current standards, 36, 41–42, 45
  and user tasks, 22, 33
  values, 23, 33
  See also FRAD; FRSAD; *individual entity names*
AustLit, 62, 68, *135, 139*
Authority
  data, 25, 26, 27, 34, 35, 50, 110, 126, 127t
  records, 6–7, 15, 25, 34, 46–50, 68, 79, 89, 98, 101, *142, 144, 145*
  See also FRAD; FRSAD

B

Benefits of FRBR, 4–8, 60
  cataloging, 6–7, 49, 51, 57, 124 (*see also* Cataloging)
  information resource management, 7–8, 57 (*see also* Resource integration)
  information retrieval systems, 4–5 (*see also* System design)
  to users, 4–5, 57
  See also individual settings; individual types of collections
Bibliographic
  data, 1–7, 28, 34, 38, 41, 44, 51, 92, 112, 130
  records, 5, 6–7, 13–15, 33–37, 46–49, 64, 67, 68 (*see also individual implementation project names*)

Bibliographic relationships, 5, 6, 15, 18–22, 26, 36, 37, 38, 42, 44, 45, 58, 60, 63, 65, 66, 67, 98, 99, 117–118
 challenges, 29–30, 43, 58–59, 102
 definition, 2
 namespaces (*see* FRBR namespace)
 treatment of (*see individual implementation project names*)
 and user tasks (*see* User tasks)
 See also FRAD; FRSAD; Relationships
BIBSYS, 42, 85, 90, 92, 93, 94, 96, 99, 100, *140*. *See also* Tool for Converting Bibliographic Records

C

Cataloging
 current practice, 3, 6, 14, 17, 45–50, 60, 65, 66, 97, 98, 102, 124
 expression-level, 37, 42, 49, 68, 103
 FRBR Delphi study, 50–51
 international principles, 3, 34 (*see also* International Cataloguing Principles)
 manifestation-level, 49, 68, 103
 standards and rules, 3, 24, 29, 34–41, 46, 50–51, 102, 124, 126, 127t, 128 (*see also individual standards names*)
 See also Benefits of FRBR; *individual collection types; individual setting types*
Cataloging rules. *See* Cataloging
CC:DA, 39, *135*
CCO, 39, 58, *135*
CDWA, 70, *135*, *143*
CIDOC, 14, *135*, *142*
CIDOC CRM, 24–25, 28, 70, *135*
Classical texts, 59, 69, 111, 125. *See also* Perseus Digital Library
Collections. *See individual collection types* (e.g., Aggregates)
Collocation, 5, 37, 42, 102–103, 111, 114, 115, 116, 117

Concept (entity), 19
Consortia, 68, 92, 93, 104, 111, 125. *See also* Union catalogs
Contextualize (user task). *See* User tasks
Conversion tool, 96, 99, 100. *See also* Tool for Converting Bibliographic Records
Corporate body (entity), 18, 19, 30
CRM. *See* CIDOC CRM
Cultural objects, 58–59, 69

D

DACS, 39, *135*
DCAM, 40, *135*
DCMI, 40, *135*. *See also* Dublin Core
DCMI/RDA Task Group, 45, *135*
*d*Collection, 69, *140*
Digital libraries, 34, 41, 68–69, 86, 102, 111, 124. *See also individual project names*
Display. *See* Interface
DLF, *135*, *140*
Dublin Core, 39, 40, 43, 45, 111, 124

E

EDItEUR, *135*. *See also* ONIX
Entities
 definition, 1, 2, 14, 25–26
 attributes (*see* Attributes)
 relationships (*see* Relationships)
 See also individual entity names
Event (entity), 19
Event modeling, 28, 62, *139*
Evergreen, 130. *See also* Open source
Expression (entity)
 attributes, 21, 29–30, 42,
 cataloging, 37, 38, 42, 46–49, 59 (*see also* Cataloging; *individual collection types*, e.g., Aggregates)
 challenges, 23–24, 29–30, 30, 43, 50, 58, 59, 60, 61, 63, 64, 65, 68, 97, 98, 101, 102
 definition, 14, 15–17, 23–24, 29

display, 94 (*see also* Interface)
and implementation projects (*see individual implementation project names; individual implementation tool names*)
See also Working Group on the Expression Entity
eXtensible Catalog (XC), 68, 86–87, 93, 130, *140*

F

Faceted display, 78, 86, 95, 112, 116, 130, *146*. *See also* Hierarchical display; Interface
Family (entity), 26
Fiction, 57, 59–61, 62, 80–81, 92, 93, 125, *139, 141*
FictionFinder, 61, 80–81, 82f, 89, 92, 93, 94, 95, 96, 113, 114, *141*
Find (user task). *See* User tasks
FRAD, 7, 26–27, 29, 35, 37, 38, 40, 50, 51, 110, 111, 124, *135*
FRANAR, 25, *136*
FRBR, *136*
    challenges (*see* Implementation: issues)
    definition, 1–3
    development, 3–4, 8–9, 23–25
    See also FRAD; FRSAD
FRBR Delphi study, 9. *See also individual FRBR areas* (e.g., Application)
FRBR display. *See* Faceted display; Hierarchical display; Interface
FRBR Display Tool, 77, 90–91, 94, 95, 96, 100–101, *141*
FRBR Floater, 91, *141*
FRBR namespace, 44–45
FRBR projects. *See individual project names*
FRBR Review Group, 6, 23–24, 45, *136*
FRBR/CRM Harmonization Group, 28, *136*

FRBR-based records, 41–42, 44, 46, 47–49, 51, 93–94, 127t, 131, *146*
FRBRization. *See* Implementation
FRBRoo, 28, *136*
FRSAD, 27, 110, 124, *136*
FRSAR, 27, 110, *136*
Full-scale systems, 76, 77–80, 96, 104, 112
FVWG, 37, 42, *136, 137*

G

GMD, 37, 44, *136*
GMD/SMD Working Group, 44, *136*
Group 1 Entities. *See* Expression; Item; Manifestation; Work
Group 2 Entities. *See* Corporate body; Family; Person
Group 3 Entities. *See* Concept; Event; Object; Place

H

Hand-press materials, 61, 125
Harmonization. *See* Models
Hierarchical catalog. *See* Hierarchical display
Hierarchical display, 5, 59, 68, 80, 87, 94, 95, 98, 102, 119, *144, 146*. *See also* Faceted display; Interface

I

ICADL, *136*
ICBC, *136*
ICOM CIDOC. *See* CIDOC
ICOM CIDOC CRM. *See* CIDOC CRM
Identify (user task). *See* User tasks
IFPA, 88–89, 96, *136, 141–142*
ILS, 87, 93, 94, *136*. *See also individual ILS names*
IME ICC, 35, 37, *137*
IMLS, *137*
Implementation
    FRBR Delphi study, 103–104
    of FRBR model, 92
    guidelines, 51, 63, 68, 70, 101–102, 125, 129

Implementation *(cont'd.)*
  issues, 60, 64, 65, 66, 67, 97–103
    (*see also* FRBR Delphi study)
  projects (*see individual project names*)
  scenarios, 49–50
  See also Open source; Software tools
INDECS, 62, *139, 142*
Information discovery, 112, 117–118,
    119, 129–130
Innovative Interfaces, 87, *136, 142*
Institutional repositories, 69, 125
Interface, 94–95
  display illustration, 78f, 79f, 80f,
    81f, 82f, 83f, 84f
  FRBR display scenarios, 49–50, 92
  issues, 5, 41, 46, 64, 98, 100–102,
    117–118
  See also Faceted display; FRBR Display
    Tool; FRBR Floater; Hierarchical
    display; User studies
International Cataloguing Principles,
    34–35, 37, 124
Internet archives, 69–70
Interoperability (data and records), 7,
    34, 51, 69, 94, 103, *139, 142*
ISADN, 27, *137*
ISBD, 3, 35–36, 39, 40, 111, 124, *137*
ISIS FRBR prototype application,
    88–89, 96, *136, 141–142*
ISSN, 25, 111, *137*
Item (entity), 14–17, 18, 23, 35, 42,
    46, 61, 62, 66, 70, 92
  attributes, 21–22 (*see also* Attributes)
  cataloging, 38, 49, 62
  definition, 14
  and implementation projects, 85,
    90, 92, *139, 140, 144, 145, 146*
    (*see also individual*
    implementation project names)
  records, 46, 47, 92

J

Justify (user task). *See* User tasks
JSC, 36–37, 44, 111, *137*
JSC FVWG. *See* FVWG

K

Kent State University FRBR Project,
    85–86, 89–90, *142*
Koha, 86, 130

L

LDOW, 44, *137*
Legacy Data, 43, 92, 94, 97–99, 131
LibDB, 89, 96, *143*
Libraries (setting), 67–68, 75–91. *See*
    also Cataloging; Implementation;
    Online catalogs
Libraries Australia FRBR Prototype.
    See LibraryLabs
Library catalogs. *See* Online catalogs
LibraryLabs, 68, 76, 82–84, 92, 93, 94,
    95, 100, 113, *143*
LibraryThing, 130
Live performances, 62–63

M

Manifestation (entity)
  attributes, 21, 30 (*see also*
    Attributes)
  cataloging, 7, 38, 41–42, 46–49, 50,
    64, 66 (*see also* Cataloging)
  challenges, 43, 58, 59, 62, 63, 64,
    66, 97, 101, 102, 118
  definition, 14, 15–17
  display (*see* Interface)
  and implementation projects (*see*
    individual implementation project
    names; individual implementation
    tool names)
  relationships, 15–17 (*see also*
    Relationships)
  See also individual collection types
    (e.g., Aggregates)
Mapping
  of FRBR elements to other standards,
    36, 37–38, 39, 43, 63, 98
  to user tasks, 26
  See also Interoperability
MARBI, 47, 49, *137*

MARC, *137*
> data, 38, 41–42, 46, 102
> FRBRization of existing MARC
>> records, 76–77, 93–94, 97–98,
>> 99, 130, 131
> and implementation projects (*see*
>> *individual implementation project*
>> *names; individual implementation*
>> *tool names*)
> and RDF, 44
> support of FRAD elements, 51 (*see*
>> *also* Mapping)
> support of FRBR elements, 41,
>> 42–43, 49 (*see also* Mapping)
Metadata. *See* Cataloging
Models
> conceptual model, 3, 14, 23, 28, 35,
>> 37, 101
> entity-relationship, 1, 14, 23
> FRBR Delphi study, 30
> object oriented, 28, 58, 70, *136*
> model interoperability, 25, 28 (*see*
>> *also* Interoperability)
> validation, 30, 113
> *See also individual model names* (e.g.,
>> FRBR)
Moving images, 58, 63–64, 93
Museums, 7, 24–25, 28, 70
Music, 64–65, 68, 83, 87, *145–146*

N

NACO, 96, *137*
Name (entity), 29
National literature, 62
NCSU, 68, *140*
NDMSO, 98, *137*
NSDL, 45, *137*

O

OAI PMH, 86, *137*
Object (entity), 1, 2, 14, 19, 58
Obtain (user task). *See* User tasks
OCLC, 61, 76, 77, *137*. *See also*
> FictionFinder; OCLC Work-Set
> Algorithm; RedLightGreen;

WorldCat
OCLC FictionFinder. *See*
> FictionFinder
OCLC Work-Set Algorithm, 61, 77, 80,
> 89–90, 94, 96, 98, 99, 100, *144*
ONIX, 44, *137, 138, 142*
Online catalogs, 5, 7, 75–86, 112–117,
> 129–130, *137*
OPAC. *See* Online catalogs
Open source, 86, 88, 89, 90, 130
OpenFRBR, 88, 92, *144*
Oral tradition works, 65–66, *137*

P

Paradigma, 69–70, *144*
Paris Principles, 3, 34–35, 40
Perseus Digital Library, 59, 69, *137,*
> *144–145*
Person (entity), 1, 2, 18, 19, 30
Place (entity), 19, 30
Prototype systems. *See individual project*
> *names*

R

RDA, 36–37, *137*
> adherence to FRBR, 38, 43, 111, 124
> issues, 38–39, 46, 60, 113
> mappings, 43, 44, 45
> registry, 40
RDA/DC Application Profile, 40, *137*
RDA/MARC Working Group, 49, *137*
RDA/ONIX, 44, *138*
RDF, 40, 44–45, 88, 89, *138*
RedLightGreen, 84–85, 92, 93, 94, 95,
> 96, *145*
Relationships
> between models, 36, 58
> *See also* Bibliographic relationships
Resource integration, 7, 129, 130
Resource description. *See* Cataloging
RICA, 40, *138*

S

SaaS, 87, *138, 146*
Search tasks. *See* User tasks

Select (user task). *See* User tasks
Serials, 24, 66–67, *140. See also*
    Aggregates
Settings. *See individual types of settings*
    (e.g., Archives)
Software tools, 8, 76–77, 86–91,
    99–101. *See also* Implementation
System design, 4, 95–96, 114–116. *See*
    also Implementation; Interface

T

Tool for Converting Bibliographic
    Records, 90, 145. *See also* BIBSYS

U

UBCIM, 25, *138*
UCLA Film and Television Archive,
    64, 76, 78–80, 93, 94, 96, *138,*
    145
Uniform titles, 17, 38, 43, 50, 60, 65
UNIMARC, 41, *138*
Union catalogs, 68, 77, 84, 92, 93. *See*
    also Consortia
URI, 38, 44, *138*
User studies, 8, 30, 86, 87, 96–97, 100,
    112–117, 126, 127t, 128–129
    FRBR Delphi study, 117–119
User tasks, 2, 23, 35
    acquire, 22, 35, 87, 114
    contextualize, 26
    explore, 28
    find, 5, 14, 22, 26, 27, 33, 87, 114
    identify, 22, 26, 27
    justify, 26
    obtain, 22, 35, 87, 114
    select, 22, 27, 81

V

Variations, 69, *145–146*
VIAF, 50, *138*
Virtua, 87, 93, *146*

VisualCat, 88, 93, *146*
VTLS, 87, 94, *138, 146*

W

W3C, 44, 96, *138*
Work (entity)
    attributes, 21, 29–30, 33
    cataloging, 51 (*see also* Authority;
        Cataloging)
    definition, 14, 29
    MARC (*see* Cataloging; MARC)
    relationships, 15–22
    RDA, 37–38
    superwork, 29, 92
    See also Aggregates; Entities
Working Group on Aggregates, 24,
    67
Working Group on Continuing
    Resources, 25
Working Group on FRANAR, 25, 27.
    See also FRANAR
Working Group on FRBR/CRM
    Dialogue, 24–25, *136*
Working Group on FRSAR. *See* FRSAR
Working Group on Subject
    Relationships, 25
Working Group on Teaching and
    Training, 25
Working Group on the Expression
    Entity, 23–24, 29, *136*
Working Group on the Future of
    Bibliographic Control, 113, 128
Works of art. *See* Cultural objects
WorldCat, 68, 77–78, 92, 93, 94, 95,
    113, 114, *146*

X

XC. *See* eXtensible Catalog
xISBN, 130
XML, 43, 51, 85, 94, 96, 100, *138*
XSLT, 94, 96, *138*

ABOUT THE AUTHORS

Yin Zhang is an Associate Professor at the School of Library and Information Science at Kent State University, Kent, Ohio. She received her BS and MS in Information Science from Wuhan University, People's Republic of China, and her PhD from the Graduate School of Library and Information Science at the University of Illinois at Urbana–Champaign. Her teaching and research areas include information organization, user information-seeking behavior, and information systems. Her articles have appeared in a variety of journals, including *Journal of the American Society for Information Science and Technology*, *Library Quarterly*, *Journal of Information Science*, and *Bulletin of the American Society for Information Science and Technology*.

Athena Salaba is an Assistant Professor at the School of Library and Information Science at Kent State University. She received her MLS from Kent State University and her PhD from the School of Library and Information Studies at the University of Wisconsin–Madison. Her research interests include organization of information, knowledge organization systems, and information-seeking behavior. She teaches courses in organization of information, cataloging and classification, metadata, and digital libraries. Dr. Salaba has a number of publications and presentations on FRSAD (Functional Requirements for Subject Authority data), FRBR (Functional Requirements for Bibliographic Records), subject access to information, and knowledge organization systems (controlled vocabularies). She is serving as the co-chair and secretary of the International Federation of Library Associations and Institutions Working Group on the Functional Requirements for Subject Authority Records (FRSAR).

Dr. Zhang and Dr. Salaba are recipients of an IMLS grant for research and development of FRBR-based systems to effectively support user tasks and information seeking. They are also the winners of the 2009 ALISE (Association for Library and Information Science Education)/Bohdan S. Wynar Research Paper Competition Award for their paper "What Is Next for FRBR? A Delphi Study," published in *Library Quarterly*.